A MICHIGAN Guide

One-Hour
Practice Tests
for the TOEFL® iBT

Lawrence J. Zwier

Lynn Stafford-Yilmaz

Editors

Ann Arbor
University of Michigan Press

Copyright © by the University of Michigan 2007
All rights reserved

ISBN-13: 978-0-472-03214-3
ISBN-10: 0-472-03214-3

Published in the United States of America
The University of Michigan Press
Manufactured in the United States of America

∞ Printed on acid-free paper

2010   2009   2008   2007   4   3   2   1

The test directions and sample questions printed in this book are not actual TOEFL® test materials. Training materials and other testing information are provided in their entirety by the University of Michigan Press. No endorsement of this publication by Educational Testing Service should be inferred.

ACKNOWLEDGMENTS

Grateful acknowledgment is made to the following authors and publishers for permission to reprint previously published materials.

The University of Michigan Press for excerpts adapted from: *Americans and Their Land: The House Built on Abundance* by Ann Mackin, copyright 2006, 1–3; *Category 5: The Story of Camille: Lessons Unlearned from America's Most Violent Hurricane* by Ernest Zebrowski and Judith A. Howard, copyright 2006, 68–69; *Deadly Dust: Silicosis and the On-Going Struggle to Protect Workers' Health, New and Expanded Edition* by David Rosner and Gerald Markowitz, copyright 2006, 49–50, 51–52; "Entertainers in the Roman Empire" by David S. Potter, in *Life, Death, and Entertainment in the Roman Empire*, edited by D. S. Potter and D. J. Mattingly, copyright © 1999, 256–57; *Free Trade and Freedom: Neoliberalism, Place, and Nation in the Caribbean* by Karla Slocum, copyright 2006, 8–10; *William G. Milliken: Michigan's Passionate Moderate* by Dave Dempsey, copyright 2006, 84–85.

The following individuals are also thanked for their contributions:

Lauren Boone and Mary Diamond for writing the sample writing responses.

Lindsay S. Devine for writing the sample speaking responses.

Matthew Rynbrandt and Kelly Sippell for writing test questions.

Kerri Kijewski for photos.

Giles Brown, Lindsay Devine, Jillian Downey, Mary Erwin, Larry Gable, Stephanie Grohoski, Deborah Kopka, Will Lovick, Joe Mooney, Brandon Naimola, Lauren Naimola, Chad Pratt, C.C. Song, and Anna Szymanski for allowing photos of themselves to appear.

Giles Brown, Lindsay Devine, Pat Grimes, Stephanie Grohoski, Chris Hebert, Badria Jazairi, Karen Pitton, Jim Reische, and Anna Szymanski for allowing their voices to appear on the audio.

Vera Irwin, Jinyun Ke, Claudio Leo, and Gad Lim for voicing sample speaking responses.

CONTENTS

To the Student   ix

To the Instructor   xi

Mini-Test 1   1

Mini-Test 2   13

Mini-Test 3   25

Mini-Test 4   39

Mini-Test 5   51

Mini-Test 6   65

Answer Key and Scoring Information (including Sample Responses)   79

Audio Transcripts   129

TO THE STUDENT

One-Hour Practice Tests for the TOEFL® iBT will help prepare you for the Internet-based TOEFL® test. This book includes six mini-tests. Each test takes about one hour. One-hour tests offer meaningful test practice in a manageable amount of time.

In most ways, the mini-tests in this book are like what you must do in the actual TOEFL®. Their content, style, and format are like those on the iBT. Both the TOEFL® iBT and these mini-tests target all four skills: reading, listening, speaking, and writing. Both use concepts from several academic fields such as biology, sociology, history, and anthropology.

Tests 1 and 2 in this book are *slightly easier* than an actual iBT. This will help you to get accustomed to TOEFL®-like questions and, in some ways, the format. It will also give you a chance to warm up your language and test-taking skills. Finally, these easier tests can help you to build stamina in using English. Many test-takers consider the iBT particularly challenging, in part because it is so long (four hours). Preparing with easier, shorter tests can help you train for the real test.

Test 3 in this book is a stepping stone. While it's not quite as easy as Tests 1 and 2, it is still close to an intermediate-level exam. Tests 4, 5, and 6 are at the same level as the actual TOEFL® iBT.

Each mini-test includes its own answer key and a scoring worksheet; all the keys and worksheets are at the back of the book. In most cases, your teacher will fill out the scoring worksheet. In other cases, you can roughly score your own answers or those of another student.

While the mini-tests in this book offer multiple advantages for test preparation, all TOEFL® takers are encouraged to take at least one full-length practice test before taking the actual test. For a full-length TOEFL® iBT, test-takers should refer to *The Michigan Guide to English for Academic Success and Better TOEFL® Test Scores*. Additionally, the publishers of the TOEFL® test offer an online version of the exam that is available at *www.ets.org/toefl/*.

Whether mini or full-length, practice tests are just one of many ways that test-takers can work toward higher TOEFL® scores. For most TOEFL® takers, scoring well on the test requires years of diligent study. Test-takers can focus their study uniquely on the TOEFL® test by studying English for academic purposes.

English for Academic Purposes emphasizes the skills needed for academic success: conventions of writing academic English, impromptu speaking on substantive topics, reading across academic disciplines, and listening to lectures on a variety of academic subjects.

One excellent resource for academic English skills is *The Michigan Guide to English for Academic Success and Better TOEFL® Test Scores*. The *Guide* contains practice in building the skills for TOEFL® success such as understanding vocabulary from context, listening for pragmatic understanding, taking notes, brainstorming, writing thesis statements, and using transitions in speech.

TO THE INSTRUCTOR

One-Hour Practice Tests for the TOEFL® iBT prepares students for the TOEFL® iBT through six mini-tests. Each can be completed in about an hour. Mini-test preparation is both effective and pragmatic. This book includes these distinctive features:

- authentic, TOEFL®-like reading and listening passages
- TOEFL®-style questions and answer options
- two lower-level, pre–iBT level tests
- one near–iBT level test that emphasizes vocabulary questions
- three iBT-level tests
- scoring sheets

The reading and listening passages in these mini-tests are substantive and engaging. They offer material you may use in your classes even beyond the tests.

Why Mini-Tests?

Many teachers want to offer realistic TOEFL® practice but cannot do it because of time constraints in their classrooms. The actual iBT takes about four hours. Few classes allow for four solid hours of testing. The teacher could assign a four-hour practice iBT for homework, but not many students have that kind of unscheduled time at home.

One-Hour Practice Tests for the TOEFL® iBT provides a flexible, academically credible solution. The mini-tests have been calibrated to condense a wide range of iBT-like tasks into about an hour.

How Does a Shorter Test Approximate a Full-Length Test?

The six mini-tests in this book reflect the content, style, and format of the actual iBT. The skills exercised—reading, listening, speaking, and writing—are the same. The number of items and their length have been adjusted to fit into a shorter time period.

These adjustments do not take away from the academically challenging nature of the reading and listening input. The reading passages are based on actual, published academic materials. They relate to the academic disciplines covered in the actual iBT, such as biology, psychology, history, and anthropology. The listening passages are likewise faithful to the content and style of those in an iBT.

To keep each mini-test to about one hour, we have made some adjustments to the time allowed for certain test items. Here are some notable timing changes:

- **Reading:** To complete each passage and its questions—18 minutes. The iBT allows 20 minutes but has from 2 to 7 more questions.

- **Listening:** To answer the questions after each listening passage—8 minutes. The passages themselves vary from about 3 to about 5 minutes, making a total of 11 to 13 minutes. The iBT does not specify a time for each listening passage, giving instead a section total of 60 to 90 minutes. This averages about 15 minutes per iBT listening passage and its questions.

- **Speaking:** For independent speaking responses—15 seconds to prepare and 45 seconds to respond. For integrated read-listen-speak responses—30 seconds to prepare and 60 seconds to respond. For integrated listen-speak responses—20 seconds to prepare and 60 seconds to respond. These are the same times as allowed on the iBT.

- **Writing:** For independent writing responses—20 minutes. For integrated writing responses—also 20 minutes. The iBT allows 30 minutes for an independent response. The shorter time in these mini-tests is necessary to keep the test as a whole close to one hour. Teachers are free to allow up to 30 minutes for an independent writing response, if they have the time.

Are These Mini-Tests as Difficult as the Real iBT?

Tests 1 and 2 are somewhat easier than the level of an actual TOEFL® test. Pre–iBT level students need to work with accessible, but still challenging, material to train for the actual test. Test 3 offers a stepping stone from the first two mini-tests to the last three. It is closer to the level of the actual iBT, but it contains fewer questions than Tests 4, 5, and 6.

Tests 4, 5, and 6 are at the same level of difficulty as the actual TOEFL®. These iBT-level tests are shorter than the four-hour test, but their language level is similar to that of an actual iBT.

How Does Practice at Different Levels Help?

Teachers and students have often approached us to complain that the iBT is too hard. Of course, we have no control over how difficult the iBT is, but we do sympathize with students who feel they are not yet ready for such a difficult test. A book that includes mini-tests at several levels provides test-preparation support for students as their academic English skills improve.

A collection of leveled tests offers multiple advantages:

- Easier tests help students build their language skills. In particular, they offer scaled practice in all four of the skill areas.

- Lower-level tests allow all students, regardless of language ability, to get more accustomed to the test format.

- Practice tests help students build stamina. One of the great challenges in a long test like the iBT is to maintain a high level of performance despite physical and mental fatigue. This requires incremental training. Just as runners do not prepare for a marathon by repeatedly running 26 miles, TOEFL® candidates should train up to the iBT with shorter tests.

How Were the Levels Created?

In leveling the material for Tests 1 and 2, we controlled several features—sentence length, number of clauses in a sentence, difficulty of vocabulary, and complexity of grammar. Also, distracting sentence elements were kept to a minimum. These include such features as parenthetical comments, phatic phrases (e.g., *not to put too fine a point on it*), chains of prepositional phrases, and editorial commentary as examples.

The reading and listening passages in Tests 1 and 2 are only about 70–80 percent as long as those in Tests 4, 5, and 6. Likewise, they offer fewer test questions per passage than the three TOEFL®-level tests. The amount of time given for the tasks, however, does not vary from level to level. We assume that students at a lower level will still find it challenging to complete shorter tasks in a standard time period.

Our leveling in these mini-tests focuses on language, not on content. We have not backed away from using substantive, academic reading and listening input at the lower level. True iBT preparation requires conceptually rich material. Where we thought there might be some hurdles, we treated them as language issues, not concept issues. For example, a student may be familiar with the heredity-versus-environment (or nature-nurture) controversy in his or her native language without recognizing it by its usual English names. In such cases, we preserved the concept, but we framed it in more accessible vocabulary.

Teachers can generally think of Tests 1 and 2 as being at a **pre–iBT** level; Test 3 at **near–iBT** level; and Tests 4, 5, and 6 **at iBT** level.

How Should I Use *One-Hour Practice Tests for the TOEFL® iBT* in My Classroom?

Students should first take one of the lower-level mini-tests. Regardless of their English language ability, students will benefit from this opportunity, and you will have some diagnostic data to work with.

After students have completed a mini-test, they should review their work. Ideally, this review should occur in the same class period as the administration of the mini-test. If this is not possible, do the review in the next class period. In your review, refer to the test's answer key and scoring information. As a class, review and discuss the correct responses. Pay particular attention to questions that were missed by several class members. As needed, return to the body of the test itself, the audio CD, or the audio transcript in order to discuss the language that is being tested.

How Can I Score the Tests?

Scoring the reading and listening sections of the TOEFL® test is a straightforward task. An answer key and a scoring worksheet are provided for each test. This worksheet guides you through the process of computing a raw score and a converted score based on the iBT scoring scale. Easy-to-use tables in the scoring worksheets give you these converted scores. While these scores can only approximate an actual iBT score, they do give a picture of how test-takers might perform on an actual iBT.

Scoring the speaking and writing sections of the test is slightly more complicated. The productive tasks, naturally, do not have right and wrong answers. Each test-taker's speaking and writing responses must be individually rated. Scoring charts for grading the four types of productive responses—independent speaking, integrated speaking, independent writing, and integrated writing—are provided as needed. Ideally, these scoring charts should be completed by English-proficient raters.

Of course, students are free to rate their own responses or those of other students, but the resulting scores are unlikely to be much like the scores an iBT rater would give.

How Should I Administer the Speaking Part of the Test?

On an actual TOEFL® test, students speak into a microphone on a headset. Each speaking response by a given student is recorded as a discrete sound file on a computer and transmitted to raters via the Internet. Few classrooms have this kind of equipment, but some alternative systems can do an adequate job.

In your classroom, you will face two main problems during the speaking section of a mini-test: (1) How can a room full of students talk simultaneously without seriously distracting each other? (2) To whom or to what will students direct their speech? Let's look at three possibilities.

1. Student-Recorder

This is by far the best option if the proper equipment is available. Each student speaks into a microphone plugged into either a tape recorder or a computer. This would work best in a language lab with a centrally controlled recording system. The student's responses could be saved either as audio files on a computer or on an audiotape for later rating.

2. Student-Teacher

In this system, the entire mini-test EXCEPT the speaking section is administered to the whole class together. Following that, the teacher schedules each student to take the speaking section individually. Unless an audio recording is made, the teacher should rate each response immediately after the student has given it. Rating from memory or even from notes is not a good idea.

3. Student-Student

Students could speak to each other and then rate each other's performances. This system is less time-consuming than the student-teacher option. Also, it will yield scores that are unlikely to be much like what iBT raters would give.

Do Mini-Tests Alone Offer Sufficient Practice for the TOEFL® Test?

While the mini-tests in this book offer multiple advantages for test preparation, all TOEFL® candidates are encouraged to take at least one full-length practice test before registering for and taking the actual iBT.

For a full-length TOEFL® or more skills practice, refer to *The Michigan Guide to English for Academic Success and Better TOEFL® Test Scores*. The guide contains practice in building skills for TOEFL® success such as understanding vocabulary from context, listening for pragmatic understanding, taking notes, brainstorming, and using transitions in speech.

Mini-Test 1

Reading

Directions: Read the passage. Answer the questions that follow. You have 18 minutes to complete the questions.

Mother of Culture

What is the nature of the relationship between a people and the land they occupy? Cultural anthropologists tell us that different cultures grow from different environmental circumstances. The land makes the man and the woman. Religious, political, and economic systems are human responses to the resources of nature. Culture results from the simple struggle to survive in a given place.

For example, let us look at the historical relationship of European Americans with their land. Theirs is an Old World culture planted in a new, uncrowded land with seemingly limitless fertile* soil, forests, water, and other natural resources. But as soon as the first European ship arrived on American shores, this meeting of people and land produced a novel interaction. It was this relation that produced the completely unique new culture of American society.

For the European settlers, home was several months away. This distance was at once frightening and empowering. Attitudes toward traditions began to transform. An independence of thought and a willingness to rethink created America as a unique political entity.

Through the years, as the people worked the land, the land worked the people. The land changed. It grew more crowded, with fewer resources. America's social and political institutions naturally adapted. Americans began to redefine their ideas about social duty and community roles. The government began to redefine its role. For example, the federal government no longer gives away free land.

*fertile: able to produce crops

Despite America's tremendous wealth, as competition for resources has increased, so have conflicts. ■1 Will we use our forests for economic purposes or for human enjoyment and wildlife? Who gets western water—farmers or city residents? ■2 Is it acceptable that our development patterns create urban settlements that are beginning to consume productive land such as farmland, timberlands, and land atop oil fields? ■3 Should a rancher own the oil, minerals, and water under the land, or is it fair for the rest of society to take what it needs from below ground? Should that rancher have the use of public land for grazing cattle that will feed other citizens? How or why should we provide affordable housing in expensive metropolitan areas? ■4

These issues require measurement of individual rights and benefits associated with land against the interests of the community. The relationship between people and their land is indeed complicated. And change in either creates change in the other, in a never-ending negotiation and renegotiation of the two entities.

1. We can infer from Paragraph 1 that the author believes

   (A) culture, as we know it, would not exist without our need for resources

   (B) the major religions are not very different from one another

   (C) culture and the land develop independently of one another

   (D) true culture can develop only after people meet their basic human needs

2. According to Paragraph 3, what effect did the American environment have on early European settlers?

   (A) It discouraged them from adapting to the new environment.

   (B) It enabled them to transplant their old culture without changing it.

   (C) It created an opportunity for changes in general attitudes.

   (D) It led them to focus on simple survival instead of cultural development.

3. As used in the passage, worked is closest in meaning to

   (A) influenced

   (B) functioned

   (C) damaged

   (D) improved

4. All of the following are mentioned in Paragraph 5 as conflicts produced by the competition for resources EXCEPT

Ⓐ the distribution of water resources

Ⓑ the need for more energy

Ⓒ building homes on fertile land

Ⓓ rights to underground resources

5. As used in the passage, consume is closest in meaning to

Ⓐ set up

Ⓑ use up

Ⓒ pay for

Ⓓ agree on

6. Look at the four squares [■] in the passage, numbered 1–4. Which square indicates the best place to insert the following sentence?

It is the balance of these conflicting ideals that has helped mold American culture.

The sentence could best be added at

Ⓐ ■1

Ⓑ ■2

Ⓒ ■3

Ⓓ ■4

7. An introductory sentence for a brief summary of the passage is given below. Complete the summary by selecting the THREE answer choices that express the most important ideas in the passage. Some answer choices do not belong because they express ideas that are not present in the passage or are minor ideas in the passage.
This question is worth 2 points.

Culture is a by-product of the human effort to use resources.

■

■

■

Answer Choices

(A) The use of natural resources in America has changed the environment and the culture of the United States.

(B) Most cultures worldwide encourage land-use practices similar to those in America.

(C) Conflicts over the land and its resources have shaped American society.

(D) The arrival of European colonists to America started a process that has produced a unique culture.

(E) The original flight of Europeans from the Old World reflected their desire for independence of thought and social organization.

Listening

 Directions: Listen to part of a lecture from a biology class. Answer the questions. Use your notes to help you. You have 8 minutes to complete the questions.

Questions about the Talk

1. What is *Drosophila melanogaster*?

   (A) a monster in a movie

   (B) a fruit fly

   (C) a scientific concept

   (D) an assumption about chromosomes

2. In the study of genetics, what does *universal* mean?

   (A) The same principles apply to all living things.

   (B) Chromosomes contain all of an organism's genes.

   (C) Similar species, like peas and apples, have similar gene structures.

   (D) The species being studied occurs around the globe.

3. Why does the lecturer mention mosquitoes and honey bees?

   (A) Genetically, they are similar to fruit flies.

   (B) They have historically been studied a lot, too.

   (C) Like fruit flies, the sequence of their genes is known.

   (D) They are small and easy to study.

4. What do we know about the life cycle of a fruit fly?
   Choose 2 answers.

   (A) Their lives are short.

   (B) It takes only two weeks for the female to lay her eggs.

   (C) Their genes change quickly from one generation to the next.

   (D) Fruit flies become adult in just 12 days.

5. Why do scientists like to study wing formation and eye color in fruit flies?

   (A) These traits are visible under a microscope.

   (B) These traits rarely vary.

   (C) The genes that affect these traits appear on all the fly's chromosomes.

   (D) These traits are not inherited in fruit flies.

Speaking

1.

Directions: Listen to the question, and then give a spoken response. You have 15 seconds to prepare your response and 45 seconds to respond. Begin preparing your response after the beep.

QUESTION

Think about the qualities of a good friend. Describe those qualities. Give specific examples and details in your response.

Preparation time: 15 seconds

Response time: 45 seconds

2.

Directions: Read a short passage on a university-related topic, and then listen to a talk on the same topic. You have 45 seconds to read the passage. The recording will be about 30 seconds in length. Respond using information from both the reading and the talk. You have 30 seconds to prepare your response and 60 seconds to respond. Begin preparing your response after the beep that follows the question.

Reading time: 45 seconds

Changes to Computer Lab Service

The university has just announced that it is planning to close two of its campus computing centers as part of a cost-reduction program. The other three campus computer labs will operate under revised schedules. The remaining centers will close at 6 PM on Friday and Saturday nights.

The university president announced that it was becoming more expensive to keep all the equipment in good working order and to operate the labs. In addition, computing centers are experiencing decreased student use as more students are coming to campus with their own computers and printers.

QUESTION

The student gives her comments on the new university policy to close computing centers or cut their hours. Summarize her opinion, and state her reasons for holding that point of view.

Preparation time: 30 seconds
Response time: 60 seconds

MINI–TEST 1

3.

Directions: Listen to a conversation between a professor and a student. Then listen to the question. Respond using information from the conversation. You have 20 seconds to prepare your response and 60 seconds to respond. Begin preparing your response after the beep.

QUESTION

Briefly describe the student's problem and the solutions that are suggested. What do you think the student should do and why?

Preparation time: 20 seconds

Response time: 60 seconds

Hw

Writing

Directions: Read the question, and then write an answer. Your answer should be about 250 words long. You have 20 minutes to plan and write your response.

QUESTION: The city has just announced that it is going to ban cell phone use in all restaurants, stores, hospitals, and other public buildings. Do you support or oppose this ban? Why?

Use specific reasons and examples to support your answer.

a timed and revised essay.

Mini–Test 2

Reading

Directions: Read the passage. Answer the questions that follow. You have 18 minutes to complete the questions.

Sand in Foundries

Foundries are factories where tools and major machine parts are made. Goods from farm machinery to iron stoves to automotive engines are cast in these plants. When most people imagine a foundry, they picture liquid metal pouring into molds of various sizes and shapes. There is intense heat from a huge furnace, and the air is heavy with fumes from lead, iron, and other metals. They also imagine scores of sweating workers laboring away. Yet perhaps the most threatening and dangerous aspect of these factories has hardly made its way into the popular imagination.

To walk into a foundry is to walk through sand. Even today, sand is used in nearly every process in a foundry. Black or green, mixed with a wide variety of other substances, scattered over the floors, the workbenches, the instruments, and the casts themselves, sand is everywhere.

■1 Foundry workers build a model of an object to be cast. They use this model as a pattern to create a sand mold. In casts that have interior openings or holes, a sand "core" is made as well. ■2 Melted metal is poured into the sand mold to create the object. ■3 After cooling, the mold and core are removed from the casting in a "shakeout"—the process of breaking up the sand mold with hammers or by mechanical vibration. ■4 After this, the castings are ready for cleaning and finishing.

Large plumes of sand dust fill the atmosphere at every foundry. The dust is usually easy to see as it floats from one part of a plant to another. Sand finds its way into every crease* in workers' clothing. When workers leave after a day's shift, they spit it from their mouths, blow it from their noses, clear it from their throats—and cough it up from their lungs.

Inhaling sand dust was understood even in the 19th century to be a danger for foundry workers. The problem grew more severe in the early 20th century as a result of fundamental changes in work methods, technology, and the organization of foundries. In the 19th century, the mixing of sand and its various binders was performed by workers using shovels, rakes, and other common hand tools. At the beginning of the 20th century, these simple tools were replaced with power tools—sand-mixers, sand-screeners, and sand-cutters—that greatly increased the amount of sand that could be mixed. These power tools also greatly increased the dust hazard that the workers were exposed to.

*crease: a small fold in fabric or paper

1. The passage portrays all of the following as dangerous aspects of foundry work EXCEPT

   Ⓐ liquid metals

   Ⓑ heat

   Ⓒ various molds

   Ⓓ fumes

2. The word fumes in the passage is closest in meaning to

   Ⓐ smelly gases

   Ⓑ poisons

   Ⓒ dust particles

   Ⓓ smoke

3. According to the passage, sand in a foundry can be

   Ⓐ black or green

   Ⓑ healthy to breathe

   Ⓒ destructive to machinery

   Ⓓ dangerous to touch

4. Look at the four squares [■] in the passage, numbered 1–4. Which square indicates the best place to insert the following sentence?

   To hold the desired shape, the sand has to be mixed with a binder—a compound that keeps the grains together.

   The sentence could best be added at

   Ⓐ ■1

   Ⓑ ■2

   Ⓒ ■3

   Ⓓ ■4

5. According to Paragraph 3, what happens to sand during the "shakeout" process?

   Ⓐ It is molded.

   Ⓑ It is removed.

   Ⓒ It is poured.

   Ⓓ It is melted.

6. The phrase the problem in Paragraph 5 refers to

   Ⓐ breathing sand dust

   Ⓑ working with sand

   Ⓒ changes in work methods

   Ⓓ dangers to foundry workers

7. An introductory sentence for a brief summary of the passage is given below. Complete the summary by selecting the THREE answer choices that express the most important ideas in the passage. Some answer choices do not belong because they express ideas that are not present in the passage or are minor ideas in the passage.
This question is worth 2 points.

One of the most common materials in a foundry—a factory that produces tools and machine parts—is sand.

- ■
- ■
- ■

Answer Choices

(A) In the 19th century, few foundry workers understood the dangers of airborne sand dust.

(B) Technological advances in foundry work have created even greater sand-dust threats to workers.

(C) Sand is used in nearly every process in a foundry, and it can be found nearly everywhere in a plant.

(D) Workers in a foundry breathe in unhealthy amounts of sand.

(E) The use of sand in present-day foundries should be reduced or even eliminated.

(F) One benefit of foundry sand is that it absorbs the toxic fumes of metals.

Listening

Directions: Listen to a conversation between two students. Answer the questions. Use your notes to help you. You have 8 minutes to complete the questions.

Questions about the Conversation

1. What does the woman want?
   - (A) sports equipment
   - (B) a place on the team
   - (C) a new I.D.
   - (D) an appointment with Charlene

2. What does the man need?
   - (A) three dollars
   - (B) the woman's name
   - (C) a student I.D. or picture I.D.
   - (D) a checklist

3. What will the woman do?

(A) go downstairs to her locker

(B) blame someone else

(C) get equipment from another office

(D) talk to Charlene

4. *Start the audio.* Listen again to part of the conversation. Then answer the question.

What does the man mean when he says, "Charlene knows everybody"?

(A) Charlene is likable.

(B) The woman is not special just because she knows Charlene.

(C) Charlene is not available.

(D) Anyone who damages equipment must see Charlene.

5. What will the man get for her?

(A) only the ball

(B) only the ball and cones

(C) only the ball and jerseys

(D) the ball, cones, and jerseys

MINI–TEST 2

Speaking

1.

Directions: Listen to the question, and then give a spoken response. You have 15 seconds to prepare your response and 45 seconds to respond. Begin preparing your response after the beep.

QUESTION

In many high schools, life-skills courses—such as money management, cooking, and basic car repair—are required. Other high schools do not require them. Should such courses be required in all high schools? Please give specific reasons to support your opinion.

Preparation time: 15 seconds

Response time: 45 seconds

2.

Directions: Read a short passage on a university-related topic, and then listen to a talk on the same topic. You have 45 seconds to read the passage. The recording will be about 30 seconds in length. Respond using information from both the reading and the talk. You have 30 seconds to prepare your response and 60 seconds to respond. Begin preparing your response after the beep.

Reading Time: 45 seconds

Heroes

A hero is someone who has done something beyond the normal range of achievement. The hero has given his or her life to something bigger than the self. Since ancient times, heroes have been central to myths and legends because their extraordinary experiences impress others. Heroes also manage to overcome their own weaknesses—pride, greed, or jealousy, for example—in order to do something good for others. There are two main types of heroic deeds. One is physical, in which the hero performs a courageous act in battle or saves a life. The other is spiritual, in which the hero experiences a deeper reality and then shares his or her message to expand the consciousness of others.

QUESTION

The professor describes some common applications of the term *hero* to real individuals. Explain the differences among a personal hero, a local hero, and a classic hero.

Preparation time: 30 seconds
Response time: 60 seconds

3.

Directions: Listen to part of a lecture from a geology class. Then listen to the question. Respond using information from the lecture. You have 20 seconds to prepare your response and 60 seconds to respond. Begin preparing your response after the beep.

QUESTION

Using information from the lecture, explain the differences among the three types of soils left by glaciers.

Preparation time: 20 seconds

Response time: 60 seconds

Writing

Directions: Read the passage. Then listen to a lecture on the same topic. You have 2 minutes to read the passage. After you have listened to the lecture, respond to the question. You have a maximum of 20 minutes to plan and write your response. Your response should be between 150 and 225 words long.

Reading Time: 2 minutes

Greek Genius

Of all that the Greeks did, only a small part has survived. What we find today is probably evidence of the highest achievement of the Greeks in various fields of thought. It is in Greek literature that we find the height of Greek philosophical and analytical achievement. Thucydides is among the great ancient historians. His *History of the Peloponnesian War* is widely considered the first work of scientific history. It describes the human world as produced by men acting from ordinary motives, without the intervention of the gods.

There is no lyrical prose that can come close to Plato's, except perhaps the Bible. Plato's writings discuss the best possible form of government. Some of his central themes are the conflict between nature and social convention. He explores the roles of nature and society on the development of human intelligence and character.

In poetry the Greeks are supreme. No epic poem can be mentioned in the same breath as Homer's *Odyssey,* celebrated for its structure and rhythm. His poetry stands alone in its time as an expression of Greek culture.

Modern societies have gained invaluable insight into Greek literature through those pieces that have survived. These are especially valuable when compared to what little is left of the Greek visual arts. The sculptures have crumbled away. The buildings are fallen now, and the paintings are gone forever. Even among writings, relatively few remain. Yet these relics are among our most precious possessions today—the legacy of Greek intellectual realization.

Listen to part of a lecture on the topic you just read about.

QUESTION: Using examples and points from the lecture and reading, explain how the priorities of Greek and Chinese civilizations influenced the achievements of each.

MINI–TEST 2

Mini-Test 3

NOTE: To give students extra practice with an important type of question, half of the reading questions relate to vocabulary.

Reading

Directions: Read the passage. Answer the questions that follow. You have 18 minutes to complete the questions.

The Caribbean Banana Industry

Around the turn of the millennium, economists and social scientists focused much attention on the Caribbean banana industry and its position in changing global markets. Several developments prompted this interest. One of them was the growth of large agribusiness* and contract farming in parts of the Caribbean. Others related to the possible loss of special trading privileges long enjoyed by Caribbean countries. These privileges usually involved preferential access to the markets of former colonial powers in Europe. Trade agreements among the countries of the European Community (EC) threatened such deals. And there was a growing belief that Latin American countries could compete better against Caribbean countries if trade protections for the latter were annulled.

■1 Many eastern Caribbean economies depended on banana exports, as they had done for nearly half a century. ■2 This raised an important question: How could economically vulnerable Caribbean farmers survive a transition to free trade? Many academic researchers worried that the enforcement of free-trade policies would lead to the destruction of Caribbean economies, livelihoods, and political interest groups.

*agribusiness: an economic sector composed of farms and farm-related operation owned by large corporations

■3 However, this focus on the global market kept observers from seeing the role of national and local forces in the global banana industry. ■4

It is easy, but not really accurate, to see globalization as an unstoppable movement. Even in high-powered economies like that of the United States, workers feel that international trade agreements have taken away their jobs. And they feel that nothing can be done to stop the rising global tide. In weaker, less-diverse economies, the damage to ordinary workers would presumably be even worse. What power would a small-scale banana farmer, for example, have against a huge American or Brazilian firm that might want to buy the farm?

In certain parts of the Windward Islands, in the southeastern Caribbean, the banana business has been completely dominated by large international companies. This has led to undesirable economic and social trends, such as outside control, political corruption, and a disregard for laborers. Elsewhere in the Caribbean, however, farm households make their own decisions without much involvement of outsiders. In short, the people in much of the Caribbean have managed to reject the domination of global corporate interests. Analysts who fail to recognize this have failed to recognize the basic interplay between the local and the global. The argument that global trade policies will wipe out local economies is far too simplistic.

1. The word preferential in the passage is closest in meaning to

   (A) extended

   (B) unfair

   (C) undeniable

   (D) favored

2. The phrase the latter in the passage refers to

   (A) the growing belief

   (B) Latin American countries

   (C) Caribbean countries

   (D) trade protections

3. The word annulled in the passage is closest in meaning to

   (A) disputed

   (B) canceled

   (C) prohibited

   (D) encouraged

MINI-TEST 3

4. The word vulnerable in the passage is closest in meaning to

  (A) easy to harm

  (B) difficult to predict

  (C) changing often

  (D) hard-working

5. Look at the four squares (■) in the passage numbered 1–4. Which square indicates the best place to insert the following sentence?

  This dependence naturally affected the lives of thousands of small-holder banana growers.

  The sentence could best to added at

  (A) ■1

  (B) ■2

  (C) ■3

  (D) ■4

6. Why does the author mention some parts of the Windward Islands?

  (A) as evidence that some communities can withstand the power of corporate domination

  (B) as a model for communities considering new free trade agreements

  (C) as an example of a place that no longer depends on banana farming

  (D) as an example of a place where global forces control a local economy

7. The word disregard in the passage is closest in meaning to

   (A) low wages

   (B) lack of vision insurance

   (C) lack of concern

   (D) illegal treatment

8. All of the following factors are mentioned in the reading as having an effect on the power of corporations in the banana business EXCEPT

   (A) the interests of the local people

   (B) local politics

   (C) regional laws

   (D) global free trade agreements

MINI–TEST 3

Listening

Directions: Listen to part of a lecture from a sociology class. Answer the questions. Use your notes to help you. You have 8 minutes to complete the questions.

Questions about the Talk

1. What is the lecture mainly about?

   Ⓐ the early history of gambling in America

   Ⓑ the funding of universities and public works in the colonies

   Ⓒ laws affecting gamblers in the New World

   Ⓓ the creation and use of lotteries in the U.S.

2. *Start the audio.* Listen again to part of the lecture. Then answer the question.

    What does the professor mean when he refers to "the Hollywood version of gambling"?

    (A) The Mississippi River valley was a dangerous place to gamble.

    (B) Motion pictures show this type of colorful, exciting gambling.

    (C) Movies were made during this time.

    (D) The games on riverboats were not true gambling.

---

3. According to the lecture, all of the following are factors that led to the end of gambling on the Mississippi EXCEPT

    (A) Citizens killed professional gamblers.

    (B) The railroad made river travel less popular.

    (C) Gambling was made illegal.

    (D) The Civil War disrupted river travel.

4. Which places are mentioned in the lecture as important centers of gambling?
Choose 2 answers.

(A) Pennsylvania

(B) Washington, DC

(C) New York

(D) New Orleans

5. According to information in the lecture, which of the following sentences best describes legal gambling in the U.S. in the mid-1800s?

(A) Most states continued to depend on lotteries to fund state government.

(B) New York's laws shaped gambling laws in other states.

(C) Most people other than the very rich had no interest in it.

(D) Most states had banned lotteries, but horse racing remained mostly legal.

Speaking

1.

Directions: Listen to the question, and then give a spoken response. You have 15 seconds to prepare your response and 45 seconds to respond. Begin preparing your response after the beep.

QUESTION

Think of experiences in your life that have taught you something you could not have learned in school. Describe one such experience, and explain how it was instructive.

Preparation time: 15 seconds

Response time: 45 seconds

2.

Directions: Read a short passage on a university-related topic, and then listen to a conversation on the same topic. You have 45 seconds to read the passage. The recording will be about 30 seconds in length. Respond using information from both the reading and the conversation. You have 30 seconds to prepare your response and 60 seconds to respond. Begin preparing your response after the beep.

Reading time: 45 seconds

Announcement from the Director of Campus Health Services

As part of this year's Keep U Healthy campaign, our month-long WalkFest event begins on Friday, November 15. All members of the university community are welcome. WalkFest will highlight the value of physical activity in ordinary daily activities, such as housecleaning, shopping, and commuting to school. Each participant will aim to walk at least three miles per day during everyday activities. All registered participants will receive a free pedometer, a WalkFest t-shirt, and a U of I water bottle. In addition, anyone attending the launching ceremony will receive a complimentary copy of the book *Walking It Off* by Dr. Ned Gammon. The launch ceremony is at noon on Friday in the Quad. Wear comfortable shoes!

QUESTION

Sue gives her opinion of walking for the school's WalkFest campaign. State her opinion and the reasons she gives for holding that opinion.

Preparation time: 30 seconds
Response Time: 60 seconds

MINI–TEST 3

3.

Directions: Listen to a conversation between two students. Then listen to the question. Respond using information from the conversation. You have 20 seconds to prepare your response and 60 seconds to respond. Begin preparing your response after the beep.

QUESTION

Briefly describe the problem and the solutions offered. What do you think the student should do and why?

Preparation time: 20 seconds

Response time: 60 seconds

Writing

Directions: Read the passage. Then listen to a lecture on the same topic. You have 2 minutes to read the passage. After you have listened to the lecture, respond to the question. You have a maximum of 20 minutes to plan and write your response. Your response should be between 150 and 225 words long.

Reading time: 2 minutes

Oatmeal's Health Benefits

Of course, eating oatmeal can influence brain function. The same could be said for any food. Foods provide the chemicals necessary for metabolism, cell replacement, and other essential bodily processes. And it stands to reason that some foods are more beneficial than others because of the nutrients they contain. Dozens of scientific studies show that oatmeal is one of the most beneficial foods for the human body. Its familiar coarse texture hints at its high-fiber content, which helps with the efficient functioning of the digestive system and thereby makes colon cancer less likely.

Oatmeal is also high in carbohydrates of the most beneficial types. These starches and complex sugars break down slowly in the body and release their energy over the course of several hours. Unlike foods containing simple sugars, which are quickly broken down, oatmeal yields a steady release of energy. This can lead to more stable moods and an ability to concentrate for longer periods. Oatmeal helps not only brain function but also the body's physical muscular functions. It's relatively low in calories, and those calories are used efficiently in metabolism.

Oatmeal contains other substances that, though less familiar, are also very beneficial. One of these is ferulic acid, which may give some protection against certain cancers—though this has not yet been shown experimentally. Ferulic acid has been definitively shown to neutralize toxins that reduce brain function. Enough ferulic acid in one's diet can keep the brain's neurons efficient. Some initial studies even show that oatmeal may be able to slow deterioration of brain function in the elderly.

 Listen to part of a lecture on the topic you just read about.

QUESTION: Summarize the points made in the lecture, explaining how they cast doubt on points made in the reading.

Mini–Test 4

Reading

Directions: Read the passage. Answer the questions that follow. You have 18 minutes to complete the questions.

Wave Patterns

Ocean waves that break on the shore are especially powerful because of the relatively sudden change of depth along the coasts. This sloping of the ocean floor redirects the wave's energy, determining how the wave will break. Water depth is just one of several variables that affect the direction and the force of a wave after it crests. To understand this, let us look at some basic features of wave formation and the behavior of waves.

On the sea, waves arise when the surface of the sea is disturbed. This disturbance could be the wind, or it could be an earth tremor, an undersea landslide, or a passing ship. As the sea bobs up and down, it transmits the disturbance to the adjacent water, which then rises and falls. This motion then sets the water further bobbing up and down, and so on.

In deep seas, the water itself moves in a vertical circle while the energy is carried horizontally as a wave. What we observe, however, is not a single set of crests and troughs but rather a complex superposition of many waves from many sources, all traveling in different directions with different heights and speeds. The sea's surface at any given moment is the sum of all the waves passing through a given point. And that pattern is continually in flux.

Blow across a loose piece of paper held in front of your lips, and the paper will rise into the air stream. A wind blowing across a sea will cause the water to rise in a hump—a hump that initiates a wave. The harder the wind blows, the faster the wave; the greater the "fetch" (the distance it blows over), the taller the wave grows.

In deep water, a wave must be extremely energetic to "break." When this does happen, the wave usually breaks backward; that is, foam and surf tumble down its backside. Thus, a ship at sea can usually survive even the worst of storms, provided that the wind and waves are traveling in the same direction (they usually do, more or less) and provided that the vessel can keep its bow* pointed into the waves. The ship then rides up the oncoming swell, over the top, and down the backside in the same direction as any breaking water. It plunges into the trough (where it may have its decks washed over as it levels out), and then rides up the next swell.

In shallow water, however, the dynamics change. ■1 A water wave carries a great deal of kinetic energy, and that energy must go somewhere. In deep water, the energy extends downward into nothing but water. ■2 When the water depth is less than about ten wavelengths (the horizontal distance between crests), the energy of the wave comes into contact with the sea floor. ■3 Now the wave drags against the bottom, its forward speed decreases, and it grows in height. ■4

All of the separate waves of different wavelengths and wave speeds now fall into a lockstep pattern, carrying their energy toward shore at one single speed. And then, when the water shallows out to where it can no longer sustain the wave's height, the wave rolls forward and breaks into an explosion of surf.

It is during its death throes, of course, that a wave does its damage. Some of it is converted into heat, a little bit goes into sound, and whatever is left goes into dislocating heavy objects it encounters—beach sand, riprap, piers, wharfs, buildings, roads, bridges, ships.

*bow: the front of a ship

1. According to Paragraph 1, which natural feature makes coastal waves powerful?

   (A) a steeply sloping sea floor

   (B) strong winds blowing toward shore

   (C) the coast's irregular shape

   (D) rapid changes in water temperature

2. The word it in the passage refers to

   (A) a wave

   (B) the surface of the sea

   (C) a disturbance

   (D) the wind

3. The word adjacent in the passage is closest in meaning to

   (A) calm

   (B) nearby

   (C) violent

   (D) deep

4. According to Paragraph 3, wave energy
   in the open sea is

   (A) diffuse

   (B) concentrated

   (C) slight

   (D) measurable

5. Why does the author recommend blowing across
   a piece on paper?

   (A) to show how air movement can initiate a wave

   (B) to demonstrate how wind speed impacts wave
   height

   (C) to illustrate the superposition of waves

   (D) to define "fetch" in visual terms

6. It can be inferred from the passage that a ship is
   unlikely to survive a storm at sea if

   (A) its bow is pointed into the waves

   (B) the wind blows in the same direction as the
   waves travel

   (C) its side faces the oncoming waves

   (D) a wave breaks near the ship

7. The word plunges in the passage is closest in meaning to

   (A) drops down

   (B) sails

   (C) capsizes

   (D) comes about

8. Look at the four squares [■] in the passage numbered 1–4. Which square indicates the best place to insert the following sentence?

   It also bends (or "refracts") until its crests are roughly parallel to the shoreline, regardless of the direction of the wind.

   The sentence could best be added at

   (A) ■1

   (B) ■2

   (C) ■3

   (D) ■4

9. The word lockstep in the passage is closest in meaning to

   (A) variable

   (B) rigid

   (C) repetitive

   (D) chaotic

10. Complete the table below by indicating which of the features of waves, according to the passage, are associated with those in open water and which are associated with those along the coast. Write the letter of each of your choices on the proper line. Two of the answer choices will not be used. **This question is worth 3 points.**

Answer Choices

(A) tend to break more powerfully

(B) tend to break backward

(C) travel in many different directions

(D) appear to be a single set of crests and troughs

(E) their motion extends all the way to the sea floor

(F) slow down and get higher

(G) break when water depth is less than about ten times the horizontal distance between crests

Waves at Sea
• _____
• _____

Waves on Shore
• _____
• _____
• _____

Listening

Directions: Listen to part of a conversation between two students. Answer the questions. Use your notes to help you. You have 8 minutes to complete the questions.

Questions about the Conversation

1. According to the woman, what was a benefit of her high school portfolio?

   (A) It forced her to organize her work.

   (B) It inspired her to save her work.

   (C) It was easy to throw away at the end of the year.

   (D) She showed it off as an example of her best work.

2. How long is the extended research paper?

   (A) 25–30 pages

   (B) 30–35 pages

   (C) 50–60 pages

   (D) 60 pages or more

3. How does the woman feel about writing a long paper?

    (A) She loves to write.

    (B) She thinks she can avoid a tough finals week.

    (C) She has an idea for an interesting topic of research.

    (D) She has already gotten a good start on the writing.

4. What does the woman say about the topic for a research paper?

    (A) A good topic justifies a longer paper; a bad one does not.

    (B) Framing the research question is the hardest part of writing.

    (C) Sometimes the professor assigns really good topics.

    (D) It's easier to cover a topic in depth rather than superficially.

5. What will the man probably do?

    (A) make a portfolio

    (B) take the final exam

    (C) write a longer research paper

    (D) research his options more

Speaking

1.

Directions: Listen to the question, and then give a spoken response. You have 15 seconds to prepare your response and 45 seconds to respond. Begin preparing your response after the beep.

QUESTION

If you could live for one year in a country other than your own, what country would it be and why?

Preparation time: 15 seconds

Response time: 45 seconds

2.

Directions: Read a short passage on a university-related topic, and then listen to a talk on the same topic. You have 45 seconds to read the passage. The recording will be about 30 seconds in length. Respond using information from both the reading and the talk. You have 30 seconds to prepare your response and 60 seconds to respond. Begin preparing your response after the beep.

Reading time: 45 seconds

Visionary Companies

The critical question asked by a visionary company is not "How well are we doing?" or "How can we do well?" or "How well do we have to perform to beat out the competition?" For these companies, the critical question is, *"How can we do better tomorrow than we did today?"* These companies institutionalize this question as a way of life—a habit of mind and action. Superb execution and performance naturally come to the visionary companies not so much as an end goal, but as the residual result of a never-ending cycle of self-stimulated improvement and investment for the future. There is no ultimate finish line in a highly visionary company. There is no point where the company feels it can live off the fruits of its labor.

QUESTION

Considering the information you have just received from the reading and the lecture, describe the characteristics of visionary companies.

Preparation time: 30 seconds
Response time: 60 seconds

3.

Directions: Listen to part of a lecture from a zoology class. Then listen to the question. Respond using information from the lecture. You have 20 seconds to prepare your response and 60 seconds to respond. Begin preparing your response after the beep.

QUESTION

Using the information presented in the lecture, describe the feeding habits of adult butterflies and butterfly larvae.

Preparation time: 30 seconds

Response time: 60 seconds

Writing

Directions: Read the question, and then write an answer. Your answer should be about 250 words long. You have 20 minutes to plan and write your response.

QUESTION: Do you agree or disagree with the following statement?

The best things in life are free.

Use specific reasons and examples to support your opinion.

Mini–Test 5

Reading

Directions: Read the passage. Answer the questions that follow. You have 18 minutes to complete the questions.

Entertainment and Values in Rome

Buildings for public entertainment remain some of the most spectacular monuments to survive from the Roman Empire, representing as they do, an enormous expenditure of society's resources on pleasure. They are a vivid reminder of the centrality of public entertainment among Rome's social values. In the Roman culture of organized public amusement, entertainment and public policy often became one and the same. The theater, amphitheater, and circus were the centers of imperial communication with the people, both in Rome and the provinces. Indeed, they became centers for the dissemination of the dominant culture.

Both the buildings and the system of entertainment were the product of long periods of evolution, representing a fusion of Italic and Greek cultural traditions. The results were not always balanced and coherent; incongruities* between the skills and the social status of different entertainers persisted throughout the centuries. Sometimes social attitudes toward different forms of entertainment mirrored the values of Greco-Roman civilization as a whole, and sometimes there was a disconnect.

incongruities: mismatches

There were, broadly speaking, four categories of public entertainer: the gymnastic, scenic, circus, and amphitheatral. Although the goal of all these subgroups was the same—to entertain the masses—the methods each used were different. Gymnastic entertainers were those whose activities were a feature of the gymnasium, the central institution of a Greek city and important in Roman cities as well. All forms of exercise were practiced there by nude gymnasts. The activities of scenic entertainers either took place within or were translated from the theater to other venues. Also included in this group are what can be termed "subtheatrical" entertainers: bear trainers, clowns, etc. Circus entertainers were, principally, chariot drivers and their assistants, though, after the beginning of the fourth century AD, most other entertainments tended to be sideshows to chariot races. Amphitheatral entertainers were those who engaged in combat with humans and beasts.

■1 Amphitheatral performers had a social status similar to that of slaves. ■2 Most of the chariot drivers in the circus were of slightly higher status and enjoyed more liberty. ■3 The most successful athletes in the Roman empire obtained membership in guilds, administered by other athletes and organized with charters that resembled Greek civic organizations. ■4 The most successful members of these associations were people of quite high status, ranking with town councilors (or mayors) in major cities. There is no logical reason why, in a society where military virtue played so important a role in national self-definition, participants in a form of entertainment that involved combat between armed humans or humans and beasts would be regarded as being of lower status than naked men who wrestled with each other.

Actors occupied a middle ground between athletes and chariot drivers or gladiators. On the one hand, some had associations; on the other hand, not all scenic performers were regarded as equally worthy. Thus, at one point some actors may be, in Rome, on a legal par with gladiators, while at another, actors of the same type might occupy the same social space as champion athletes. Much of this variability can be attributed to frequent shifts in Roman attitudes toward theatrical works themselves. When plays were considered a form of art, actors benefited. When plays were seen as, essentially, a frivolous waste of time, actors fell from favor.

1. According to Paragraph 1, what did places of public entertainment represent in the Roman provinces of ancient times?

    (A) a center for the distribution of Roman ideals

    (B) an evolution of Italic and Greek culture

    (C) an expensive place where people could vote on policy

    (D) a merging of public policy and imperial communication

2. As used in the passage, persisted is closest in meaning to

    (A) convinced

    (B) remained

    (C) evolved

    (D) decreased

3. The word there in the passage refers to

    (A) Roman cities

    (B) Greek cities

    (C) the gymnasium

    (D) the empire

4. All of the following were forms of entertainment based primarily on skills of physical strength or speed EXCEPT

(A) gymnastic

(B) scenic

(C) circus

(D) amphitheatral

---

5. We can infer from Paragraph 4 that membership in a guild or association was considered to be

(A) a sign of corruption

(B) a way to enter political office

(C) worthy of respect

(D) proof of land ownership

---

6. Look at the four squares [■] in the passage numbered 1–4. Which square indicates the best place to insert the following sentence?

The relative standing of these different groups defined a wide, and not always stable, range.

The sentence could best be added at

(A) ■ 1

(B) ■ 2

(C) ■ 3

(D) ■ 4

7. Which of the following best expresses the essential information of the highlighted sentence? Incorrect choices change the meaning in important ways or leave out essential information.

(A) It is hard to understand why a military-oriented society ranked combat entertainers lower than wrestlers.

(B) A society that values military skills as highly as it honors performing arts shows contradictions.

(C) Entertainment involving combat between armed humans and/or beasts is common in a society that defines itself by its military strength.

(D) On logic alone, one would expect a military-oriented society to be tired of symbols of combat and therefore to shun military-focused hobbies.

8. As used in the passage, par is closest in meaning to

(A) level

(B) competition

(C) disparity

(D) dispute

9. As used in the passage, frivolous is closest in meaning to

(A) entertaining

(B) expensive

(C) healthy

(D) silly

10. An introductory sentence for a brief summary of the passage is given below. Complete the summary by selecting the THREE answer choices that express the most important ideas in the passage. Some answer choices do not belong because they express ideas that are not present in the passage or are minor ideas in the passage. This question is worth 2 points.

This passage explains that public entertainment in ancient Rome was a focal point of its public and political culture.

- ■
- ■
- ■

Answer Choices

(A) The complicated system of entertainment in ancient Rome bore a resemblance to both Italic and Greek cultural traditions.

(B) At the core of all Roman policy and political decisions were the great venues of entertainment which were scattered about the ancient Roman world.

(C) Public entertainment was broken into four distinct groups, each of which had its own niche in society.

(D) Gladiators and chariot drivers were of lower status than athletes, despite the Roman respect for military accomplishment.

(E) Scenic performers had a shifting status somewhere between the charioteers and the athletes, depending on prevailing attitudes toward the theater.

Listening

Directions: Listen to part of a lecture and discussion from a health class. Answer the questions. Use your notes to help you. You have 8 minutes to complete the questions.

Questions about the Talk

1. What is the lecture mainly about?

   (A) the process of food irradiation

   (B) radioactive waste produced in irradiation facilities

   (C) extension of irradiation to medical and dental industries

   (D) purposes of food irradiation

2. What is a "cobalt pencil"?

   (A) a rechargeable storage device for cobalt

   (B) a reactor where cobalt is manufactured

   (C) a by-product of manufacturing nuclear weapons

   (D) a way of recycling cobalt as a writing tool

3. What major differences does the professor point out between cobalt and cesium?
Choose 2 answers.

(A) Cesium produces less-powerful radiation.

(B) Cesium has a longer half-life.

(C) Cesium is a powder, and cobalt is a solid metal.

(D) The only U.S. cesium reactor is in Georgia.

4. *Start the audio.* Listen again to part of the lecture. Then answer the question.

What does the lecturer mean when she says, "We're getting a little off track here"?

(A) The cesium transport vehicle got off track.

(B) She has gotten onto a topic that isn't her main topic.

(C) She's running out of time.

(D) Irradiation of food and irradiation of medical and dental products are different processes.

5. Complete the chart by putting an X in the appropriate boxes according to the information given in the lecture.

	Gamma Rays	Electron Beams	X-Rays
Penetrates thicker foods			
Leaves radioactive waste			
Propels beams at a target			
Uses a thin plate of gold or other metal			

6. According to the lecturer, why isn't X-ray irradiation more common?

(A) It's expensive.

(B) It offers limited penetration.

(C) It melts packaging materials with metal content.

(D) It's a newer technology.

Speaking

1.

Directions: Listen to the question, and then give a spoken response. You have 15 seconds to prepare your response and 45 seconds to respond. Begin preparing your response after the beep.

QUESTION

Some volunteer work involves doing something directly for *people*, such as teaching someone to read or serving food. Other volunteers work mostly with *things*, such as preparing mailings or working on computers. What type of volunteer work do you prefer, and why? Give reasons to support your answer.

Preparation time: 15 seconds
Response time: 45 seconds

2.

> **Directions:** Read a short passage on a university-related topic, and then listen to a conversation on the same topic. You have 45 seconds to read the passage. The recording will be about 30 seconds in length. Respond using information from both the reading and the conversation. You have 30 seconds to prepare your response and 60 seconds to respond. Begin preparing your response after the beep.

Reading time: 45 seconds

Reading Requirement for Incoming Freshmen

In our effort to make your first year as educational as possible, we are requiring all incoming freshman to read the novel *The Namesake* by Jhumpa Lahiri. The novel explores the life of an Indian man, including a decision he makes as a young college student. The book deals with the theme of living in a new country and with many diverse cultures. The university believes that this requirement will assist you with your adjustment to life on campus.

You are expected to complete your reading before freshman orientation. The university will provide opportunities for group discussions on the novel during orientation week.

QUESTION

Briefly describe the woman's view of the reading requirement and the topics that she expects to be discussed.

Preparation time: 30 seconds
Response time: 60 seconds

3.

Directions: Listen to a conversation between a professor and a student. Then listen to the question. Respond using information from the conversation. You have 20 seconds to prepare your response and 60 seconds to respond. Begin preparing your response after the beep.

QUESTION

Briefly describe the student's problem and the solutions that are suggested. What do you think the student should do and why?

Preparation time: 20 seconds
Response time: 60 seconds

Writing

Directions: Read the question, and write an answer. Your answer should be about 250 words long. You have 20 minutes to plan and write your response.

QUESTION: The earth is warming, due partly to emissions from human activities that use fossil fuels. Besides changing our driving patterns, what daily lifestyle changes do you think humans could make to reduce their consumption of fossil fuels?

Use specific reasons and examples to support your opinion.

Mini–Test 6

Reading

Directions: Read the passage. Answer the questions that follow. You have 18 minutes to complete the questions.

Governor Milliken and DDT

William Milliken came to office in 1969, at a time when the national and state environmental crisis was reaching a new level of seriousness, triggering a public clamor for action. On June 22, 1969, the oil-slicked Cuyahoga River caught fire at Cleveland, resulting in national publicity that helped create momentum for the federal Clean Water Act of 1972. ■1 Michigan was far from immune to pollution problems. Black plumes of smoke were a typical sight in the state's industrial cities, especially in the downriver area of Detroit. ■2 The Rouge River often ran orange or black with the wastes dumped by Ford Motor Company, and hundreds of miles of Lake Michigan swimming beaches were considered unfit for public use at times because of high bacteria counts. ■3 Chemical plants in Midland, Muskegon, and elsewhere were fouling the rivers and lakes with dioxin and other carcinogens. ■4

Most significantly, in Milliken's first spring as governor, a long-running battle over the use of the toxic pesticide DDT in Michigan was coming to a boil. In the late 1950s, an ornithologist at Michigan State University, Dr. George Wallace, had documented significant bird die-offs on campus resulting from high concentrations of the DDT used to treat Dutch elm disease. In Rachel Carson's landmark 1962 book *Silent Spring*, Wallace's research was cited, contributing to fears of a world characterized by "a strange stillness . . . a spring without voices." Citizens and civic groups, including the League of Women Voters, rallied across the state against DDT use and formed the Michigan Pesticides Council, a volunteer group committed to the eradication of DDT and other so-called hard pesticides. This class of chemicals was new to the world.

Unlike most natural substances, the hard pesticides take hundreds of years to break down, and they accumulate in the fat of animals, including humans, posing health risks scientists were struggling to define.

But the chemical industry that manufactured the pesticides, and the agricultural sector that used them, defended DDT and other chemicals, claiming that they represented the best hope of promoting farm productivity and the health of trees and other organisms afflicted by pests. Some public-health experts warned that, without DDT, viral encephalitis and other temperate-zone diseases borne* by mosquitoes, fleas, and ticks would run rampant. One horticulturalist urged Americans "to accept some injury to restricted segments of our wildlife population in return for the irrefutably better standard of living we now enjoy because of agricultural chemicals." During most of the 1960s in Michigan, citizens fought the farm interests, and natural resource agencies warred with agricultural agencies.

Then came a startling discovery that doomed DDT in Michigan and put it on the road to elimination in the United States. The U.S. Food and Drug Administration (FDA) routinely examined interstate shipments of coho salmon, a large fish with significant stores of fat that was initially stocked in Lake Michigan in 1966 by the Michigan Department of Conservation. During one of the inspections, the FDA found high levels of DDT and seized 14 tons of fish. At around the same time, the Michigan Department of Agriculture (MDA) detected another pesticide, dieldrin, and impounded 500,000 pounds of salmon. These discoveries generated front-page headlines across Michigan and threatened Michigan's thriving new Great Lakes sport fishery. With the health of the tourism industry—as well as the people who ate the fish—at risk, the state's agricultural commission banned most uses of DDT in April 1969, making Michigan the first state to do so.

*borne: carried

1. The word clamor in the passage is closest in meaning to

   (A) initiative

   (B) demand

   (C) debate

   (D) inquiry

2. Why does the author mention the Cuyahoga and Rouge rivers?

   (A) to illustrate the impact of hard pesticides on bodies of water

   (B) as examples of issues that led to Milliken's election

   (C) to show that pollution can spread far from its source

   (D) as examples of environmental crises in the late 1960s

3. Look at the four squares [■] in the passage numbered 1–4. Which square indicates the best place to insert the following sentence?

   This profusion of environmental bad news would spawn a heated debate about public priorities in the state of Michigan.

   The sentence could best be added at

   (A) ■ 1

   (B) ■ 2

   (C) ■ 3

   (D) ■ 4

MINI-TEST 6

4. Why does the author use the phrase *coming to a boil* in the passage?

   (A) to hint at the threat posed by global warming

   (B) to indicate that a long controversy was becoming a crisis

   (C) to emphasize Milliken's growing anger over environmental damage

   (D) to refer to the effects that chemical pollutants have on bodies of water

5. What can be inferred from Paragraph 2 about Rachel Carson's book?

   (A) It shows how huge populations of bacteria had damaged the habitats of other animals.

   (B) It mentions attempts by state officials to silence Dr. Wallace.

   (C) It deals partly with the possibility that bird populations were being devastated.

   (D) It suggests that animals harmed by DDT were losing the ability to vocalize.

6. The word they in the passage refers to

   (A) DDT and other chemicals

   (B) the agricultural sector

   (C) organisms affected by pesticides

   (D) the chemical industry

7. According to Paragraph 3, the chemical industry believed that

(A) some environmental risk was acceptable because DDT was so beneficial

(B) citizens should oppose efforts by farm owners to stop the use of DDT

(C) reports of environmental harm caused by DDT were totally false

(D) citizens should accept a lower standard of living to prevent environmental damage

8. The word impounded in the passage is closest in meaning to

(A) destroyed

(B) confiscated

(C) inspected

(D) weighed

9. All of the following are mentioned in the passage as being true of Michigan's tourism industry in the late 1960s EXCEPT

(A) The ban on DDT was instituted partly to protect it.

(B) Its sport-fishing segment was experiencing strong growth in the late 1960s.

(C) It was threatened by highly publicized discoveries of DDT and dieldrin in fish.

(D) Governmental support for it was withdrawn after the discovery of DDT in fish.

10. Complete the table below by indicating which of the listed items, according to the passage, benefit from the use of DDT and which are harmed by it. Write the letter of each of your choices on the proper line. TWO of the answer choices will NOT be used. **This question is worth 4 points.**

Answer Choices

(A) potential victims of viral encephalitis

(B) elm trees

(C) the Cuyahoga River

(D) chemical companies

(E) animals that eat salmon

(F) Milliken's election campaign

(G) birds

(H) farm productivity

(I) Michigan's tourism industry

Positively Affected by DDT Use
• _____
• _____
• _____
• _____

Negatively Affected by DDT Use
• _____
• _____
• _____

Listening

Directions: Listen to part of a lecture from a psychology class. Answer the questions. Use your notes to help you. You have 8 minutes to complete the questions.

Questions about the Talk

1. What is subliminal perception?

   (A) an ability to sense what happens while one sleeps

   (B) the conscious perception of stimuli

   (C) ideas that a person carries subconsciously

   (D) the subconscious awareness of stimuli

2. Why does the lecturer mention the story of the marketer who said that a theater sold more popcorn and soda when these words were shown subliminally during the movie?

(A) to give evidence that subliminal messages influence consumers' behavior

(B) to show why researchers need to be cautious about their initial findings

(C) to show that many marketing specialists use subliminal messages

(D) to demonstrate that some popular beliefs about subliminal perception are false

3. *Start the audio.* Listen again to part of the lecture. Then answer the question.

What does the lecturer imply when he says, "I hope I haven't wrecked any of your plans"?

(A) Self-help tapes are an important tool in changing negative behaviors.

(B) People who plan to lose weight by listening to tapes will probably not succeed.

(C) Positive thinking is more important than subliminal tapes in losing weight.

(D) Self-help tapes about smoking and weight loss are more effective when they contain subliminal messages.

4. What does the boy do with the cake in one study by Morris Eagle?
   Choose 2 answers.

   Ⓐ tosses it

   Ⓑ eats it

   Ⓒ offers it

   Ⓓ makes it

5. According to the lecturer, one study has shown that subliminal stimuli

   Ⓐ can influence buying decisions

   Ⓑ can affect people's actions

   Ⓒ cannot have any influence on people

   Ⓓ can have a subtle, short-lived impact on perceptions

6. Which statement best explains the *mere exposure effect*?

   Ⓐ People have a better opinion of shapes they have seen before.

   Ⓑ People recognize shapes they have seen before.

   Ⓒ Repeated exposure to a shape causes people to perceive it in different ways.

   Ⓓ Viewing a shape subliminally helps people learn the shape.

Speaking

1.

Directions: Listen to the question, and then give a spoken response. You have 15 seconds to prepare your response and 45 seconds to respond. Begin preparing your response after the beep.

QUESTION

Many companies now allow their employees to telecommute and work from home. If you were given this option, would you choose to work from home or go into the office to work? Give reasons to support your answer.

Preparation time: 15 seconds

Response time: 45 seconds

2.

Directions: Read a short passage on a university-related topic, and then listen to a talk on the same topic. You have 45 seconds to read the passage. The recording will be about 30 seconds in length. Respond using information from both the reading and the talk. You have 30 seconds to prepare your response and 60 seconds to respond. Begin preparing your response after the beep.

Reading time: 45 seconds

The Right to Privacy

About 100 years ago, U.S. Supreme Court Justice Louis D. Brandeis called the right to privacy "the right to be let alone." Eloquent in its simplicity, this phrase seems to sum up what most Americans have in mind when they think of privacy. However, legally, it offers no guidance at all. Wanting privacy as a right is one thing, but is there any real reason to think that we legally have such a right? In fact, the word *privacy* does not appear in the U.S. Constitution. In asserting a right to privacy, jurists have based their reasoning mostly on the Fourth Amendment to the Constitution, which states in part, "The right of the people to be secure in their persons, houses, papers, and effects, against unreasonable searches and seizures, shall not be violated." Since 1923, the Supreme Court has interpreted this amendment to mean that, in most cases, people can marry, raise children, conduct their family lives, and seek or refuse medical help as they see fit, without the threat of government interference.

QUESTION

Considering the information you have just received from the reading and the lecture, describe the right to privacy and some conflicts related to it.

Preparation time: 30 seconds
Response time: 60 seconds

3.

Directions: Listen to part of a lecture from a history class. Then listen to the question. Respond using information from the talk. You have 20 seconds to prepare your response and 60 seconds to respond. Begin preparing your response after the beep.

QUESTION

Using the information presented in the lecture, describe the relationship between Roosevelt and Churchill, and say why it was important.

Preparation time: 20 seconds
Response time: 60 seconds

Writing

Directions: Read the passage. Then listen to a lecture on the same topic. You have 2 minutes to read the passage. After you have listened to the lecture, respond to the question. You have a maximum of 20 minutes to plan and write your answer. Your response should be between 150 and 225 words long.

Reading time: 2 minutes

The American legal system is a prime example of trying to solve problems through adversarial procedures—by pitting two sides against each other and letting them slug it out in public. It reflects and reinforces our assumptions that truth emerges when two polarized, warring extremes are set against each other. While it might seem harsh, it has worked well for more than 200 years.

Perhaps the best thing about adversarial procedures is that they require disputing parties to clarify their positions before a judge or jury even hears the case. Exactly which points are under dispute? What have previous court cases said about similar disputes? The issues must be framed in terms that relate directly to points of law and to previous cases. Emotional disputes from contested divorces to business-fraud cases have to be made less emotional. Documentation is required, not just heartfelt pleading. This may not be emotionally satisfying to the parties involved, but it allows an impartial outside judge to see through to the heart of the matter.

Some of the most basic principles of law can only be satisfied through adversarial procedures. In criminal cases, for example, the government brings charges against a person and that person has a chance to stand up in court and challenge them. This puts the citizen in an adversarial position with regard to the government, and this a very good thing for the defendant. The government has to expose its case to public challenges. At least in theory, there cannot be any unchallenged secret charges or back-room convictions. Adversarial systems ensure that matters truly public are tried in public, and that judgments are recorded objectively to inform future cases.

A system that replaced adversarial procedures with negotiations would be very unfair to the least powerful members of society. They have hardly any leverage. How could they effectively negotiate with the state or with a giant corporation? Granted, some negotiation occurs even in our adversarial system. A criminal plea-bargains with the government. The criminal agrees to plead guilty to a lesser charge, saving the government time and money and getting reduced prison time in return. Adversaries in a civil suit agree to compromise. But none of these negotiations would be possible if a lengthy, costly adversarial procedure did not loom over both parties.

Listen to part of the lecture on the topic you just read about.

QUESTION: Summarize the points made in the lecture, explaining how they cast doubt on points made in the reading.

ANSWER KEY AND SCORING INFORMATION (INCLUDING SAMPLE RESPONSES)

Mini–Test 1

Reading (page 1)

1. A. culture, as we know it, would not exist without our need for resources
2. C. It created an opportunity for changes in general attitudes.
3. A. influenced
4. B. the need for more energy
5. B. use up
6. D. ■ 4
7. (summary)
   - A. The use of natural resources in America has changed the environment and the culture of the United States.
   - C. Conflicts over the land and its resources have shaped American society.
   - D. The arrival of European colonists to America started a process that has produced a unique culture.

Reading: Scoring Information

■ For each of the six multiple-choice questions, a correct answer ➔ 1 point.
■ For Question 7 (summary):
   all three answers chosen correctly ➔ 2 points
   only two correct ➔ 1 point
   fewer than two correct ➔ 0 points

Total possible in reading section: 8

Add your points. This is your raw score. Use the conversion table to convert your raw score to one similar to a TOEFL® score.

Reading Score Conversion	
Raw Score	Converted Score
8	30
7	25
6	19
5	14
4	9
3	4
2	1
1	0
0	0

Your Score for Reading: _____

Listening (page 6)

1. B. A fruit fly
2. A. The same principles apply to all living things.
3. C. Like fruit flies, the sequence of their genes is known.
4. A. Their lives are short.
   D. Fruit flies become adults in just 12 days.
5. A. These traits are visible under a microscope.

Listening: Scoring Information

■ For each of the five questions, a correct answer ➜ 1 point. In Questions 2 and 4, the answers must be entirely correct to earn a point.

Total possible in listening section: 5

Add your points. This is your raw score. Use the conversion table to convert your raw score to one similar to a TOEFL® score.

Listening Score Conversion	
Raw Score	Converted Score
5	30
4	22
3	14
2	6
1	0
0	0

Your Score for Listening: _____

Speaking (page 8)

Rate each element of the response using the scoring charts. Then follow the directions to estimate your score.

Question 1: Friend (independent speaking task)

Is there a clear statement of the main idea?	0	1	2	3	4
Are there specific ideas that support the main idea?	0	1	2	3	4
Are the ideas organized logically?	0	1	2	3	4
Is the information relevant and complete?	0	1	2	3	4
Is the grammar understandable and correct?	0	1	2	3	4
Is vocabulary correct and varied?	0	1	2	3	4
Is pronunciation clear and understandable?	0	1	2	3	4
Is the speech smooth and flowing?	0	1	2	3	4

This speaking question is worth 4 points. Add your points from each row. Divide the total by 8. Round to the nearest half-point; for scores ending in .25 or .75, round up.

Question 1 Raw Score: _____ (0–4)

Question 2: Computer Lab (integrated speaking task)

Is there a clear statement of the main idea or an organizing statement?	0	1	2	3	4
Does the speaker incorporate information from both the reading and the listening?	0	1	2	3	4
Does the speaker give an accurate summary of the student's opinions and her reasons?	0	1	2	3	4
Does the speaker use time effectively?	0	1	2	3	4
Is the grammar understandable and correct?	0	1	2	3	4
Is vocabulary correct and varied?	0	1	2	3	4
Is pronunciation clear and understandable?	0	1	2	3	4
Is the speech smooth and flowing?	0	1	2	3	4

This speaking question is worth 4 points. Add your points from each row. Divide the total by 8. Round to the nearest half-point; for scores ending in .25 or .75, round up.

Question 2 Raw Score: _____ **(0–4)**

Question 3: Change Majors (integrated speaking task)

Is there a clear statement of the main idea or an organizing statement?	0	1	2	3	4
Does the speaker accurately describe?	0	1	2	3	4
Does the speaker use time effectively?	0	1	2	3	4
Is the grammar understandable and correct?	0	1	2	3	4
Is vocabulary correct and varied?	0	1	2	3	4
Is pronunciation clear and understandable?	0	1	2	3	4
Is the speech smooth and flowing?	0	1	2	3	4

This speaking question is worth 4 points. Add your points from each row. Divide the total by 7. Round to the nearest half-point; for scores ending in .25 or .75, round up.

Question 3 Raw Score: _____ **(0–4)**

Add your raw scores for the three speaking questions. Round up for any half points. (For example, 9.5 becomes 10.) Your raw score will be between 0 and 12 points. Use the conversion table to convert your raw score to one similar to a TOEFL® score.

Speaking Score Conversion	
Raw Score	**Converted Score**
12	30
11	27
10	24
9	20
8	18
7	15
6	12
5	9
4	5
3	2
2	1
1	0
0	0

Your Score for Speaking: _____

Sample responses can be heard on the audio CD (Tracks 33–35). Transcripts of these responses follow.

Question 1. Um, a good friend is someone who you not only have things in common with, but who also has your best interest at heart, and is a good and loyal person. However, uh, being loyal doesn't always mean . . . just blindly, just taking your friend's side; it means supporting them through both good and bad times, and helping them regain perspective if they're about to make a bad choice or life decision. Good friends have fun together, and bring out each other's good qualities. Sometimes we develop, uh, superficial relationships, friendships with people that are fun for a while, but they don't often, um, really last.

Question 2. The student who called the comment line is not happy about the University's decision to close computing labs and cut the hours of the ones that are remaining. She says she understands that the school is trying to save money, but she also makes a point that they are doing so in a way that makes the students pay, and it's especially unfair to the students with less money and who have access to their own printers and computer equipment. One of her points is that students need to use the labs for printing papers and assignments. She says that under the current schedule, students already have to wait to print things. She says that the students with enough money to buy their own printers can solve their problem that way, but that students—uh, other students who can't afford that—are being put at a disadvantage by the University's policy. It sounds like she herself does not own a printer, and so she's concerned on her own behalf as well as others'.

Question 3. Um, this student is not entirely sure what she wants to get her degree in. Uh, she's consulting her journalism professor because she found, um, that she liked her journalism classes better than her teacher education classes. Becoming a teacher was, uh, was her original plan, but now she is trying to learn more about careers in journalism. She's afraid of the cost of changing majors, that it will be more expensive because she'll have to stay in school longer. And her professor, um, she asks her, what she really wants to do. One of her suggestions is, to um, is for her to double major and to finish both degrees . . . or to just finish her teaching degree first and then go to the night school. She also says she could do an internship at a newspaper to see if she, if she likes journalism.

Writing *(page 11)*

Rate each element of the response using the scoring chart. Then follow the directions to estimate your score.

Independent writing task

Is there a clear thesis statement?	0	1	2	3	4	5
Are there specific ideas that support the thesis?	0	1	2	3	4	5
Are the ideas organized logically?	0	1	2	3	4	5
Is the information relevant and complete?	0	1	2	3	4	5
Are sentences grammatically correct using a variety of sentence types?	0	1	2	3	4	5
Is vocabulary correct and appropriate to the topic?	0	1	2	3	4	5
Are transitions logical and smooth?	0	1	2	3	4	5

This writing question is worth 5 points. Add your points from each row. Divide the total by 7. Round to the nearest half-point; for scores ending in .25 or .75, round up.

Use the conversion table to convert your raw score to one similar to a TOEFL® score.

Writing Score Conversion	
Raw Score	**Converted Score**
5.0	30
4.5	26
4.0	22
3.5	20
3.0	17
2.5	13
2.0	8
1.5	3
1.0	1
0	0

Your Score for Writing: _____

A sample response follows.

Cell phone use in public places is rude. To make themselves heard, people talking on cell phones often have to shout. This disturbs others near them. Also, it can be embarrassing to listen in on half of a phone conversation. You might hear details about someone's business or personal life that you would rather not hear. Yet you have no choice when someone three feet from you is shouting them out.

Talking on the phone in a restaurant is particularly rude—unless the talker is dining alone. You go with other people to a restaurant so you can socialize with them. If you're talking on a cell phone, you are not paying attention to your companions. In addition, waiters at restaurants are unable to do their jobs smoothly when diners spend their time on cell phones. Waiters know how to avoid interrupting customers in face-to-face conversations. With cell phones, none of the usual clues are apparent. And other people in the restaurant will enjoy their meals less because cell phone conversations around them are ruining the atmosphere.

In other places like a hospital, cell phone use should be banned because of the danger. Most hospitals do ban them now. This is because a cell phone could interfere with medical equipment, such as the machines that read a patient's heartbeat. Also, a doctor might be distracted by cell phones ringing and people talking on them. A doctor's complete attention is needed to ensure the safety of everyone. If a doctor is distracted by a conversation, he or she may accidentally listen and might make a mistake. A patient's life could depend on the doctor's attention.

New cell-phone technology is making the problem even worse. Now, you can get cell phones that fit over one ear and have a microphone pointing at your mouth. You don't even need to use your hands. People wearing cell phones like this seem to be talking to themselves, so you wonder if there's something wrong with them. Or you might hear that person's voice and think he or she is talking to you.

(339 words)

Total Score

Add the four converted scores: reading, listening, speaking, and writing. The TOEFL® iBT is worth 120 points. _____

Mini–Test 2

Reading (page 13)

1. C. various molds
2. A. smelly gases
3. A. black or green
4. B. ■2
5. B. It is removed.
6. A. breathing sand dust
7. (summary)
   - B. Technological advances in foundry work have created even greater sand-dust threats to workers.
   - C. Sand is used in nearly every process in a foundry, and it can be found nearly everywhere in a plant.
   - D. Workers in a foundry breathe in unhealthy amounts of sand.

Reading: Scoring Information

- For each of the six multiple-choice questions, a correct answer → 1 point.
- For Question 7 (summary):
  all three answers chosen correctly → 2 points
  only two correct → 1 point
  fewer than two correct → 0 points

Total possible in reading section: 8

Add your points. This is your raw score. Use the conversion table to convert your raw score to one similar to a TOEFL® score.

Reading Score Conversion	
Raw Score	**Converted Score**
8	30
7	25
6	19
5	14
4	9
3	4
2	1
1	0
0	0

Your Score for Reading: _____

Listening (page 18)

1. A. sports equipment
2. C. a student I.D. or picture I.D.
3. A. go downstairs to her locker
4. B. The woman is not special just because she knows Charlene.
5. B. only the ball and cones

Listening: Scoring Information

■ For each of the five questions, a correct answer ➔ 1 point.

Total possible in listening section: 5

Add your points. This is your raw score. Use the conversion table to convert your raw score to one similar to a TOEFL® score.

Listening Score Conversion	
Raw Score	**Converted Score**
5	30
4	22
3	14
2	6
1	0
0	0

Your Score for Listening: _____

Speaking (page 20)

Rate each element of the response using the scoring charts. Then follow the directions to estimate your score.

Question 1: Life-Skills Classes (independent speaking task)

Is there a clear statement of the main idea?	0	1	2	3	4
Are there specific ideas that support the main idea?	0	1	2	3	4
Are the ideas organized logically?	0	1	2	3	4
Is the information relevant and complete?	0	1	2	3	4
Is the grammar understandable and correct?	0	1	2	3	4
Is vocabulary correct and varied?	0	1	2	3	4
Is pronunciation clear and understandable?	0	1	2	3	4
Is the speech smooth and flowing?	0	1	2	3	4

This speaking question is worth 4 points. Add your points from each row. Divide the total by 8. Round to the nearest half-point; for scores ending in .25 or .75, round up.

Question 1 Raw Score: _____   (0–4)

Question 2: Heroes (integrated speaking task)

Is there a clear statement of the main idea or an organizing statement?	0	1	2	3	4
Does the speaker incorporate information from both the reading and the listening?	0	1	2	3	4
Does the speaker give an accurate summary of the information?	0	1	2	3	4
Does the speaker use time effectively?	0	1	2	3	4
Is the grammar understandable and correct?	0	1	2	3	4
Is vocabulary correct and varied?	0	1	2	3	4
Is pronunciation clear and understandable?	0	1	2	3	4
Is the speech smooth and flowing?	0	1	2	3	4

This speaking question is worth 4 points. Add your points from each row. Divide the total by 8. Round to the nearest half-point; for scores ending in .25 or .75, round up.

Question 2 Raw Score: _____   (0–4)

Question 3: Soils (integrated speaking task)

Is there a clear statement of the main idea or an organizing statement?	0	1	2	3	4
Does the speaker give an accurate summary of the information?	0	1	2	3	4
Does the speaker use time effectively?	0	1	2	3	4
Is the grammar understandable and correct?	0	1	2	3	4
Is vocabulary correct and varied?	0	1	2	3	4
Is pronunciation clear and understandable?	0	1	2	3	4
Is the speech smooth and flowing?	0	1	2	3	4

This speaking question is worth 4 points. Add your points from each row. Divide the total by 7. Round to the nearest half-point; for scores ending in .25 or .75, round up.

Question 3 Raw Score: _____ (0–4)

Add your raw scores for the three speaking questions. Round up for any half points. (For example, 9.5 becomes 10.) Your raw score will be between 0 and 12 points. Use the conversion table to convert your raw score to one similar to a TOEFL® score.

Speaking Score Conversion	
Raw Score	**Converted Score**
12	30
11	27
10	24
9	20
8	18
7	15
6	12
5	9
4	5
3	2
2	1
1	0
0	0

Your Score for Speaking: _____

Sample responses can be heard on the audio CD (Tracks 36–38). Transcripts of these responses follow.

Question 1. I think that all high schools should require life-skills classes. How to cook and how to manage money are things that some students maybe can learn at home. But not everyone's parents have those skills, or the parents might not . . . take time at home to teach these, these things to their children. For example, I think my parents managed their money pretty well, but they never talked about it with me. And having required classes at high schools will make sure that everybody has the same good education in cooking, car repair, and house repair. It will pre-pare people for leaving home after they graduate.

Question 2. The professor describes a "personal hero" as some, as some-body you admire. There is an example of Tiger Woods . . . a personal hero could be an athlete, or musician, or just someone you like and respect. Then she describes "local hero" as a person whom people living in a certain region respect and love, but maybe not everyone does. The example here is Napoleon. He was a hero to the people in France. But the people that he was attacking wouldn't call him "hero." The "real heroes," in comparison to the local heroes, are the ones who . . . have a pure reason behind what they're doing. They are doing something great and making a sacrifice, and they're not selfish as people. Like Gandhi and Mother Teresa, they are above ordinary humans, and they are hard to find in real life.

Question 3. Soils that were moved around and then left by glaciers can be of three different types. The first type, till soil, does not hold so much water close to the surface, so the plants don't have much time to absorb the water. These plants have to . . . uh, uh, live without water pretty often. Other soil, with some clay or silt in it, keeps more water near the surface, but does not stay too wet. The last soil type, with a lot of clay, holds the most water, and so a whole forest of trees and smaller plants can grow here because they have enough water available to them. Different kinds of plant communities need these different kinds of soil, but all types of soil can grow plants.

Writing (page 23)

Rate each element of the response using the scoring chart. Then follow the directions to estimate your score.

Integrated writing task

	0	1	2	3	4	5
Does the response do what the prompt asks for?	0	1	2	3	4	5
Is there a clear thesis statement?	0	1	2	3	4	5
Are there specific ideas that support the thesis?	0	1	2	3	4	5
Does the writer incorporate information from both the reading and the lecture?	0	1	2	3	4	5
Does the writer accurately interpret information from the reading and lecture?	0	1	2	3	4	5
Are the ideas organized logically?	0	1	2	3	4	5
Is the information relevant and complete?	0	1	2	3	4	5
Are sentences grammatically correct using a variety of sentence types?	0	1	2	3	4	5
Is vocabulary correct and appropriate to the topic?	0	1	2	3	4	5
Are transitions logical and smooth?	0	1	2	3	4	5

This writing question is worth 5 points. Add your points from each row. Divide the total by 10.

Raw Score: _____ (0–5)

Use the conversion table to convert your raw score to one similar to a TOEFL® score.

Writing Score Conversion	
Raw Score	**Converted Score**
5.0	30
4.5	26
4.0	22
3.5	20
3.0	17
2.5	13
2.0	8
1.5	3
1.0	1
0	0

Your Score for Writing: _____

A sample response follows.

Greek civilization and Chinese civilization both made significant contributions to history. The Greeks made achievements in philosophy and in literature and history. The Chinese contributed to human progress by developing ink, porcelain, and other practical things like better navigation. The difference in the kinds of contributions each made relates to their different world views.

According to the lecture, the Greeks' belief in man's ability to control his destiny influenced them to record their stories in now famous histories and to philosophize about their importance in the universe. Their work focuses on the thoughts and experiences of individuals. Because many Greek accomplishments were written or recited works, many have been lost.

The Chinese, on the other hand, placed a cultural emphasis on harmony. They developed practical items that would contribute to a productive, balanced society. Because of this different focus, the Chinese led the world in development of technological advances like irrigation systems and navigation techniques for trade. These practical designs were less likely to get lost than the Greek achievements were.

The author and speaker also both mention the number and quality of the contributions of the Greeks and the Chinese. Together they both praise both cultures, but the speaker makes it clear that the Chinese contributed more and more useful developments to history than the Greeks did.

(218 words)

Total Score

Add the four converted scores: reading, listening, speaking, and writing. The TOEFL® iBT is worth 120 points.

Your Score for Mini–Test 2 _____

Mini–Test 3

Reading (page 25)

1. B. unfair
2. C. Caribbean countries
3. B. canceled
4. A. easy to harm
5. ■ 2
6. D. as an example of a place where global forces control a local economy
7. C. lack of concern
8. C. regional laws

Reading: Scoring Information

- For each of the six multiple-choice questions, a correct answer → 1 point.
- For Question 7 (summary):
  all three answers chosen correctly → 2 points
  only two correct → 1 point
  fewer than two correct → 0 points

Total possible in reading section: 8

Add your points. This is your raw score. Use the conversion table to convert your raw score to one similar to a TOEFL® score.

Reading Score Conversion	
Raw Score	**Converted Score**
8	30
7	25
6	19
5	14
4	9
3	4
2	1
1	0
0	0

Your Score for Reading: _____

Listening (page 30)

1. A. the early history of gambling in America
2. B. Motion pictures show this type of colorful, exciting gambling.
3. C. Gambling was made illegal.
4. C. New York
   D. New Orleans
5. D. Most states had banned lotteries, but horse racing remained mostly legal.

Listening: Scoring Information

■ For each of the five questions, a correct answer ➔ 1 point. In Question 4, the answer must be entirely correct to earn a point.

Total possible in listening section: 5

Add your points. This is your raw score. Use the conversion table to convert your raw score to one similar to a TOEFL® score.

Listening Score Conversion	
Raw Score	**Converted Score**
5	30
4	22
3	14
2	6
1	0
0	0

Your Score for Listening: _____

Speaking (page 33)

Rate each element of the response using the scoring charts. Then follow the directions to estimate your score.

Question 1: Life Experience (independent speaking task)

Is there a clear statement of the main idea?	0	1	2	3	4
Are there specific ideas that support the main idea?	0	1	2	3	4
Are the ideas organized logically?	0	1	2	3	4
Is the information relevant and complete?	0	1	2	3	4
Is the grammar understandable and correct?	0	1	2	3	4
Is vocabulary correct and varied?	0	1	2	3	4
Is pronunciation clear and understandable?	0	1	2	3	4
Is the speech smooth and flowing?	0	1	2	3	4

This speaking question is worth 4 points. Add your points from each row. Divide the total by 8. Round to the nearest half-point; for scores ending in .25 or .75, round up.

Question 1 Raw Score: _____ **(0–4)**

Question 2: WalkFest (integrated speaking task)

Is there a clear statement of the main idea or an organizing statement?	0	1	2	3	4
Does the speaker incorporate information from both the reading and the listening?	0	1	2	3	4
Does the speaker give an accurate summary of the woman's opinion and her reasons?	0	1	2	3	4
Does the speaker use time effectively?	0	1	2	3	4
Is the grammar understandable and correct?	0	1	2	3	4
Is vocabulary correct and varied?	0	1	2	3	4
Is pronunciation clear and understandable?	0	1	2	3	4
Is the speech smooth and flowing?	0	1	2	3	4

This speaking question is worth 4 points. Add your points from each row. Divide the total by 8. Round to the nearest half-point; for scores ending in .25 or .75, round up.

Question 2 Raw Score: _____ **(0–4)**

Question 3: Problem with CD (integrated speaking task)

Is there a clear statement of the main idea or an organizing statement?	0	1	2	3	4
Does the speaker accurately describe the problem and solutions?	0	1	2	3	4
Does the speaker use time effectively?	0	1	2	3	4
Is the grammar understandable and correct?	0	1	2	3	4
Is vocabulary correct and varied?	0	1	2	3	4
Is pronunciation clear and understandable?	0	1	2	3	4
Is the speech smooth and flowing?	0	1	2	3	4

This speaking question is worth 4 points. Add your points from each row. Divide the total by 7. Round to the nearest half-point; for scores ending in .25 or .75, round up.

Question 3 Raw Score: _____ **(0–4)**

Add your raw scores for the three speaking questions. Round up for any half points. (For example, 9.5 becomes 10.) Your raw score will be between 0 and 12 points. Use the conversion table to convert your raw score to one similar to a TOEFL® score.

Speaking Score Conversion	
Raw Score	**Converted Score**
12	30
11	27
10	24
9	20
8	18
7	15
6	12
5	9
4	5
3	2
2	1
1	0
0	0

Your Score for Speaking: _____

Sample responses can be heard on the audio CD (Tracks 39–41). Transcripts of these responses follow.

Question 1. Um, having pets, um, had taught me a lot that you can't learn from books in school. It taught me how to take care of something else that's living . . . and how to be responsible for it. When I was little I had a fish that I fed every morning. And then later, my family found a cat that was lost near a busy road, and we took her home, took her to the vet, and, um, we got her a collar and tags. Taking care of any animal requires a lot of work. Over time, I got, I got more cats and other pets, too. I became very responsible and also learned so much about relating to animals. I could have never learned these things in school. Now, because of this experience, I think I will even be a better parent.

Question 2. The woman says that she does not care about sports and exercise, and she thinks that the WalkFest at the school is ridiculous. The campaign says that people exercise while doing daily activities like cleaning and shopping. The woman thinks that it cannot be possible for her to walk three miles a day. Her other reason is that she likes to wear shoes that match her clothes . . . for her it's more important having her shoes match than getting some exercise. The WalkFest organizers are offering some free gifts, like a book or a pedometer, but she doesn't want them. And to make a final excuse, she says she has a class at the same time as the WalkFest event. There isn't one thing that interests her for about the WalkFest.

Question 3. The problem the student has is that the computer will not read the CD she bought. When she tried to use the CD, the computer screen went blank, and then it was hard to get the CD out. Uh, at first the person working thinks that it . . . that um, that she doesn't have the right computer and that's why the CD wouldn't work. But it says the CD works with her computer, so then he thinks maybe the CD is broken. He says, uh, he can give her another CD to try. Or he can test the CD to see if there is anything wrong with it, and if not, then she needs to have her computer repaired. . . . I think she needs to wait for him to test the CD because if her computer is broken, then maybe any CD would get stuck in there, and, uh, she needs to have it fixed anyway. Also, um, she won't waste time trying another CD.

Writing (page 36)

Rate each element of the response using the scoring chart. Then follow the directions to estimate your score.

Integrated writing task

Does the response do what the prompt asks for?	0	1	2	3	4	5
Is there a clear thesis statement?	0	1	2	3	4	5
Are there specific ideas that support the thesis?	0	1	2	3	4	5
Does the writer incorporate information from both the reading and the lecture?	0	1	2	3	4	5
Does the writer accurately interpret information from the reading and lecture?	0	1	2	3	4	5
Are the ideas organized logically?	0	1	2	3	4	5
Is the information relevant and complete?	0	1	2	3	4	5
Are sentences grammatically correct using a variety of sentence types?	0	1	2	3	4	5
Is vocabulary correct and appropriate to the topic?	0	1	2	3	4	5
Are transitions logical and smooth?	0	1	2	3	4	5

This writing question is worth 5 points. Add your points from each row. Divide the total by 10.

Raw Score: _____ (0–5)

Use the conversion table to convert your raw score to one similar to a TOEFL® score.

Writing Score Conversion	
Raw Score	**Converted Score**
5.0	30
4.5	26
4.0	22
3.5	20
3.0	17
2.5	13
2.0	8
1.5	3
1.0	1
0	0

Your Score for Writing: _____

A sample response follows.

Both sources report that oatmeal is a healthy food for most people, but the lecture casts doubt on the claims of the reading by suggesting that the claims in the reading are exaggerated. According to the lecture, oatmeal is not the miracle food some have claimed that it is.

The lecturer admits that oatmeal does contain nutrients and fiber. The lecturer also adds that oatmeal has the appeal of being inexpensive and easy to prepare. But despite its benefits, the lecturer points out that the oatmeal diets of the 1980s were deceptive. The people who promoted these diets wanted only to sell products related to the diet plans, not really to treat or cure people's illnesses.

In fact, the lecturer points out that people with gluten allergies might become more ill if they eat large quantities of oatmeal. The lecturer also reminds listeners that eating large quantities of any food can cause excessive weight gain, a health problem of its own. So the claims of the reading have to be put into context. Eating oatmeal will probably not bring dramatic mental and physical health improvements. The only two points that the reading and lecture agree on are that oatmeal contains nutrients and that it is high in fiber.

(208 words)

Total Score

Add the four converted scores: reading, listening, speaking, and writing. The TOEFL® iBT is worth 120 points. _____

Mini–Test 4

Reading (page 39)

1. A. a steeply sloping sea floor
2. C. a disturbance
3. B. nearby
4. A. diffuse
5. A. to show how air movement can initiate a wave
6. C. its side faces the oncoming waves
7. A. drops down
8. D. ■ 4
9. B. rigid
10.

Waves at Sea
• B. tend to break backward
• C. travel in many different directions
Waves on Shore
• A. tend to break more powerfully
• E. their motion extends all the way to the sea floor
• F. they slow down and get higher

Reading: Scoring Information

■ For each of the nine multiple-choice questions (Questions 1 through 9), a correct answer ➜ 1 point.
■ For Question 10 (completing a table):
   all five answers chosen correctly ➜ 3 points
   only four correct ➜ 2 points
   only three correct ➜ 1 point
   fewer than three correct ➜ 0 points

Total possible in reading section: 12

Add your points. This is your raw score. Use the conversion table to convert your raw score to one similar to a TOEFL® score.

Reading Score Conversion	
Raw Score	**Converted Score**
12	30
11	27
10	24
9	20
8	18
7	15
6	12
5	9
4	5
3	2
2	1
1	0
0	0

Your Score for Reading: _____

Listening (page 45)

1. B. It inspired her to save her work.
2. C. 50–60 pages
3. B. She thinks she can avoid a tough finals week.
4. A. A good topic justifies a longer paper; a bad one does not.
5. B. take the final exam

Listening: Scoring Information

■ For each of the five multiple-choice questions, a correct answer ➔ 1 point.

Total possible in listening section: 5

Add your points. This is your raw score. Use the conversion table to convert your raw score to one similar to a TOEFL® score.

Listening Score Conversion	
Raw Score	Converted Score
5	30
4	22
3	14
2	6
1	0

Your Score for Listening: _____

Speaking (page 47)

Rate each element of the response using the scoring charts. Then follow the directions to estimate your score.

Question 1: Living in Another Country (independent speaking task)

Is there a clear statement of the main idea?	0	1	2	3	4
Are there specific ideas that support the main idea?	0	1	2	3	4
Are the ideas organized logically?	0	1	2	3	4
Is the information relevant and complete?	0	1	2	3	4
Is the grammar understandable and correct?	0	1	2	3	4
Is vocabulary correct and varied?	0	1	2	3	4
Is pronunciation clear and understandable?	0	1	2	3	4
Is the speech smooth and flowing?	0	1	2	3	4

This speaking question is worth 4 points. Add your points from each row. Divide the total by 8. Round to the nearest half-point; for scores ending in .25 or .75, round up.

Question 1 Raw Score: _____ **(0–4)**

Question 2: Visionary Companies (integrated speaking task)

Is there a clear statement of the main idea or an organizing statement?	0	1	2	3	4
Does the speaker incorporate information from both the reading and the listening?	0	1	2	3	4
Does the speaker give an accurate summary of the information?	0	1	2	3	4
Does the speaker use time effectively?	0	1	2	3	4
Is the grammar understandable and correct?	0	1	2	3	4
Is vocabulary correct and varied?	0	1	2	3	4
Is pronunciation clear and understandable?	0	1	2	3	4
Is the speech smooth and flowing?	0	1	2	3	4

This speaking question is worth 4 points. Add your points from each row. Divide the total by 8. Round to the nearest half-point; for scores ending in .25 or .75, round up.

Question 2 Raw Score: _____ (0–4)

Question 3: Butterflies (integrated speaking task)

Is there a clear statement of the main idea or an organizing statement?	0	1	2	3	4
Does the speaker give an accurate summary of the information?	0	1	2	3	4
Does the speaker use time effectively?	0	1	2	3	4
Is the grammar understandable and correct?	0	1	2	3	4
Is vocabulary correct and varied?	0	1	2	3	4
Is pronunciation clear and understandable?	0	1	2	3	4
Is the speech smooth and flowing?	0	1	2	3	4

This speaking question is worth 4 points. Add your points from each row. Divide the total by 7. Round to the nearest half-point; for scores ending in .25 or .75, round up.

Question 3 Raw Score: _____ (0–4)

Add your raw scores for the three speaking questions. Round up for any half points. (For example, 9.5 becomes 10.) Your raw score will be between 0 and 12 points. Use the conversion table to convert your raw score to one similar to a TOEFL® score.

Speaking Score Conversion	
Raw Score	Converted Score
12	30
11	27
10	24
9	20
8	18
7	15
6	12
5	9
4	5
3	2
2	1
1	0
0	0

Your Score for Speaking: _____

Sample responses can be heard on the audio CD (Tracks 42–44). Transcripts of these responses follow.

Question 1. If I could live for one year in another country, I would choose a country most people don't think of—Luxembourg. I think this would be a great place to live. It's a very small country, so I could really get to know it well in one year. I could travel around, and, um, I could also travel to other countries very easily, since it's right between, um, Germany, France, and Belgium. . . . Uh, Luxembourg would also be a wonderful place to learn languages because they speak three different languages there—German, French, and, um, their own dialect. You are exposed to all of them at once and I think it would be a fascinate, fascinating place to live.

Question 2. A visionary company is a special kind of company . . . a kind that wants to never stop improving. This is different from the traditional company because, uh, the traditional company might have a goal, uh, to make a certain amount of money, or to only improve certain things. But the visionary company's only goal is to always do better, in every way. Visionary companies are always thinking about the future, and specifically . . . uh, about how they can do better in the future than they are doing today. We know that they really do think more about the future than traditional companies because of the financial research, which tells us that the visionary companies spend more money on new equipment and put more money back into the company. They are willing to spend more on training and educating their employees, too. And they are much faster than traditional companies in picking up new technology. So a visionary company always thinks ahead, and it doesn't limit itself with smaller goals.

Question 3. Adult butterflies have different feeding habits from butterfly larvae. It is important for the adults to have a variety of different kinds of plants to eat. But the larvae will eat only one kind of plant. There is research about why the offspring eat differently than the mother. The scientists thought that the reason could be genetic, or that the different plants could produce chemicals that stop the larvae from eating. But it only has to do with which plant the eggs are laid on. Whatever plant the eggs developed on, the larvae will eat it, even if the plant produces chemicals that should make the larvae not want to eat it. The chemicals are not poisonous, and if the egg was laid there, . . then it seems that the larvae is already used to it, and can eat the plant.

Writing (page 50)

Rate each element of the response using the scoring chart. Then follow the directions to estimate your score.

Independent writing task

Is there a clear thesis statement?	0	1	2	3	4	5
Are there specific ideas that support the thesis?	0	1	2	3	4	5
Are the ideas organized logically?	0	1	2	3	4	5
Is the information relevant and complete?	0	1	2	3	4	5
Are sentences grammatically correct using a variety of sentence types?	0	1	2	3	4	5
Is vocabulary correct and appropriate to the topic?	0	1	2	3	4	5
Are transitions logical and smooth?	0	1	2	3	4	5

This writing question is worth 5 points. Add your points from each row. Divide the total by 7. Round to the nearest half-point; for scores ending in .25 or .75, round up.

Raw Score: _____ (0–5)

Use the conversion table to convert your raw score to one similar to a TOEFL® score.

Writing Score Conversion	
Raw Score	**Converted Score**
5.0	30
4.5	26
4.0	22
3.5	20
3.0	17
2.5	13
2.0	8
1.5	3
1.0	1
0	0

Your Score for Writing: _____

A sample response follows.

I disagree with the statement that the best things in life are free. People who believe that are not paying attention to the costs of the things they like to do. It's true that we get the most joy from things you cannot buy in a store, like love, friendship, or happiness. But even though these things are not for sale, they are not free.

If you think carefully about love, you'll see it isn't free. To get into situations where you can experience love, you need money. Going on a date is expensive. And if your dates go well and you wish to marry, you need a lot of money. In my country, a man must have a good job and money before any woman would agree to marry him. If you do get married and you want to enjoy the love between a parent and a child, you need money. Trying to raise children without enough money will only bring heartbreak to you and your family. No parent wants to see his or her children hungry, or sick, or uneducated, or without decent clothes. Unfortunately, parents with too little money see this all the time.

Friendship is not free either. You build friendships by doing things with other people. You don't just hang out at somebody's house and do nothing. You go with your friends to movies, bars, sporting events, and so on. Maybe you have to buy equipment that will help you share activities, like mountain bikes or golf clubs. If you have no money to do things with them, my friends will think I am boring. Money is important in keeping friendships.

Finally, happiness is not free. You cannot be happy without marriage and friends. A poor person is not happy, because he or she is always worried about having money, paying rent, and buying food. Poor people cannot travel or do fun things. You cannot buy happiness, but having money can make happiness a lot easier to find.

(332 words)

Total Score

Add the four converted scores: reading, listening, speaking, and writing. The TOEFL® iBT is worth 120 points. _____

Mini–Test 5

Reading (page 51)

1. A. a center for the distribution of Roman ideals
2. B. remained
3. C. the gymnasium
4. B. scenic
5. C. worthy of respect
6. A. ■ 1
7. A. It is hard to understand why a military-oriented society ranked combat entertainers lower than wrestlers.
8. A. level
9. D. silly
10. • C. Public entertainment was broken into four distinct groups, each of which had its own niche in society.
    • D. Gladiators and chariot drivers were of lower status than athletes, despite the Roman respect for military accomplishment.
    • E. Scenic performers had a shifting status somewhere between the charioteers and the athletes, depending on prevailing attitudes toward the theater.

Reading: Scoring Information

■ For each of the nine multiple-choice questions (Questions 1 through 9), a correct answer → 1 point.
■ For Question 10 (summary):
  all three answers chosen correctly → 2 points
  only two correct → 1 point
  fewer than two correct → 0 points

Total possible in reading section: 11

Add your points. This is your raw score. Use the conversion table to convert your raw score to one similar to a TOEFL® score.

Reading Score Conversion	
Raw Score	**Converted Score**
11	30
10	27
9	23
8	20
7	17
6	14
5	10
4	6
3	2
2	1
1	0
0	0

Your Score for Reading: _____

Listening (page 57)

1. A. the process of food irradiation
2. A. a rechargeable storage device for cobalt
3. B. Cesium has a longer half-life.
   C. Cesium is a powder, and cobalt is a solid metal.
4. B. She has gotten onto a topic that isn't her main topic.
5.

	Gamma Rays	Electron Beams	X-Rays
Penetrates thicker foods	X		X
Leaves radioactive waste	X		
Propels beams at a target		X	X
Uses a thin plate of gold or other metal			X

6. D. It's a newer technology.

Listening: Scoring Information

■ For each of the six questions, a correct answer ➜ 1 point.

Total possible in listening section: 6

Add your points. This is your raw score. Use the conversion table to convert your raw score to one similar to a TOEFL® score.

Listening Score Conversion	
Raw Score	**Converted Score**
6	30
5	23
4	17
3	9
2	3
1	0
0	0

Your Score for Listening: _____

Speaking (page 60)

Rate each element of the response using the scoring charts. Then follow the directions to estimate your score.

Question 1: Volunteer Work (independent speaking task)

Is there a clear statement of the main idea?	0	1	2	3	4
Are there specific ideas that support the main idea?	0	1	2	3	4
Are the ideas organized logically?	0	1	2	3	4
Is the information relevant and complete?	0	1	2	3	4
Is the grammar understandable and correct?	0	1	2	3	4
Is vocabulary correct and varied?	0	1	2	3	4
Is pronunciation clear and understandable?	0	1	2	3	4
Is the speech smooth and flowing?	0	1	2	3	4

This speaking question is worth 4 points. Add your points from each row. Divide the total by 8. Round to the nearest half-point; for scores ending in .25 or .75, round up.

Question 1 Raw Score: _____ (0–4)

Question 2: Reading Requirement (integrated speaking task)

Is there a clear statement of the main idea or an organizing statement?	0	1	2	3	4
Does the speaker accurately describe the problem and solutions?	0	1	2	3	4
Does the speaker use time effectively?	0	1	2	3	4
Is the grammar understandable and correct?	0	1	2	3	4
Is vocabulary correct and varied?	0	1	2	3	4
Is pronunciation clear and understandable?	0	1	2	3	4
Is the speech smooth and flowing?	0	1	2	3	4

This speaking question is worth 4 points. Add your points from each row. Divide the total by 8. Round to the nearest half-point; for scores ending in .25 or .75, round up.

Question 2 Raw Score: _____ (0–4)

Question 3: Poli-Sci Class (integrated speaking task)

Is there a clear statement of the main idea or an organizing statement?	0	1	2	3	4
Does the speaker give an accurate summary of the information?	0	1	2	3	4
Does the speaker use time effectively?	0	1	2	3	4
Is the grammar understandable and correct?	0	1	2	3	4
Is vocabulary correct and varied?	0	1	2	3	4
Is pronunciation clear and understandable?	0	1	2	3	4
Is the speech smooth and flowing?	0	1	2	3	4

This speaking question is worth 4 points. Add your points from each row. Divide the total by 7. Round to the nearest half-point; for scores ending in .25 or .75, round up.

Question 3 Raw Score: _____ **(0–4)**

Add your raw scores for the three speaking questions. Round up for any half points. (For example, 9.5 becomes 10.) Your raw score will be between 0 and 12 points. Use the conversion table to convert your raw score to one similar to a TOEFL® score.

Speaking Score Conversion	
Raw Score	**Converted Score**
12	30
11	27
10	24
9	20
8	18
7	15
6	12
5	9
4	5
3	2
2	1
1	0
0	0

Your Score for Speaking: _____

Sample responses can be heard on the audio CD (Tracks 45–47). Transcripts of these responses follow.

Question 1. I personally like to volunteer and work with people, instead of things, but I think both can be important. I used to volunteer at a summer camp in my town doing art and music activities with the kids. Working with children, I could watch them learn and grow. I got to know their likes and dislikes and skills. That personal interaction is, it's what I enjoy in my work. But there were also volunteers at the camp working on computers in the office. Without them, we couldn't keep records of the kids' name, address, and any al-, medication or allergy . . . those kinds of things. If you are working for a valuable goal, the type of work is not important.

Question 2. The woman is happy and excited about the reading requirement. The woman thinks the book will help them discuss differences in race, religion, and economic groups, and she thinks it will help prepare her for college. Uh, the man she's talking to is not comfortable talking about those things because he thinks someone may be offended by the discussion . . . if it is too close to their own situation. The woman thinks that people in college are able to handle that discussion and that the discussion will, will help her adapt to college life.

Question 3. Uh, the student's problem is that she wants to take a class—Poli-Sci 312—but she needs permission of the instructor. She is talking to the 12, uh, 312 instructor, asking about permission and prerequisites. She wants to skip the prerequisites, because first, um, she says that she had a background of studying American history and French politics. Second, she also wants to start in Poli-Sci 312 this semester because she wants to take the 411 series of classes the next year, so she must finish the 300-level classes this year. I think the student needs to just look honestly at the topics in the class syllabus, um, that the professor gives her. If she is really comfortable and has some background knowledge on those subjects, then she should go back and ask the professor to sign her up for the class. But if she has never studied those topics before, she should really wait and take the 311 class first.

Writing (page 63)

Rate each element of the response using the scoring chart. Then follow the directions to estimate your score.

Independent writing task

Is there a clear thesis statement?	0	1	2	3	4	5
Are there specific ideas that support the thesis?	0	1	2	3	4	5
Are the ideas organized logically?	0	1	2	3	4	5
Is the information relevant and complete?	0	1	2	3	4	5
Are sentences grammatically correct using a variety of sentence types?	0	1	2	3	4	5
Is vocabulary correct and appropriate to the topic?	0	1	2	3	4	5
Are transitions logical and smooth?	0	1	2	3	4	5

This writing question is worth 5 points. Add your points from each row. Divide the total by 7. Round to the nearest half-point; for scores ending in .25 or .75, round up.

Raw Score: _____ (0–5)

Use the conversion table to convert your raw score to one similar to a TOEFL® score.

Writing Score Conversion	
Raw Score	**Converted Score**
5.0	30
4.5	26
4.0	22
3.5	20
3.0	17
2.5	13
2.0	8
1.5	3
1.0	1
0	0

Your Score for Writing: _____

A sample response follows.

How can we reduce the use of fossil fuels? Other than changing our driving behaviors, there are three main ways to do this. First, people can adjust what they're wearing so that it keeps them warm or cool. People can wear more or fewer clothes rather than turning up the heat or turning up the air conditioner. Where winters are cold, people can wear several layers of clothes even while indoors, reducing the need to use fossil fuel-generated power to heat their homes. People in warmer climates can wear fewer clothes to remain cool.

A second way to reduce the use of fossil fuels by individuals is to reduce the amount of electricity used every day in one's workplace. For instance, turning off an office light and a computer when they are not needed can reduce a person's use of electricity. Since most of the electricity used in the United States comes from burning fossil fuels, less electricity use means less fuel use. Workers should also avoid making unnecessary photocopies, opening the office refrigerator for no reason, or using the office coffee-maker too much. These may seem like small things, but they add up.

Finally, people can reduce their use of fossil fuels by buying local products. If everyone bought only local goods, the need for fossil fuels for transportation of products could be reduced. Stores that saw an increase in the sales of local products would buy more from local producers and less from far away. Fewer trucks would be driving across several states to supply these stores. The amount of fossil fuel necessary to get food from a farm to your table would decrease.

Changing one's driving behaviors is the most obvious way for an individual to reduce her use of fossil fuels, but it is not the only way. Practical clothing, energy conservation, and reduced importation of outside products can also contribute.

(315 words)

Total Score

Add the four converted scores: reading, listening, speaking, and writing. The TOEFL® iBT is worth 120 points. _____

Mini–Test 6

Reading (page 65)

1. B. demand
2. D. as example of environmental crises in the late 1960s
3. ■ 4
4. B. to indicate that a long controversy was becoming a crisis
5. C. It deals partly with the possibility that bird populations were being devastated.
6. A. DDT and other chemicals
7. A. Some environmental risk was acceptable because DDT was so beneficial.
8. B. confiscated
9. D. Governmental support for it was withdrawn after the discovery of DDT in fish.
10.

Positively Affected by DDT Use
• A. potential victims of viral encephalitis
• B. elm trees
• D. chemical companies
• H. farm productivity

Negatively Affected by DDT Use
• E. animals that eat salmon
• G. birds
• I. Michigan's tourism industry

Reading: Scoring Information

■ For each of the nine multiple-choice questions (Questions 1 through 9), a correct answer ➜ 1 point.
■ For Question 10 (completing a table):
all seven answers chosen correctly ➜ 4 points
only six answers correct ➜ 3 points
only five answers correct ➜ 2 points
only four answers correct ➜ 1 point
fewer than four answers correct ➜ 0 points

Total possible in reading section: 13

Add your points. This is your raw score. Use the conversion table to convert your raw score to one similar to a TOEFL® score.

Reading Score Conversion	
Raw Score	**Converted Score**
13	30
12	28
11	25
10	21
9	19
8	16
7	13
6	10
5	7
4	4
3	2
2	1
1	0
0	0

Your Score for Reading: _____

Listening (page 71)

1. D. the subconscious awareness of stimuli
2. D. to demonstrate that some popular beliefs about subliminal perception are false
3. B. People who plan to lose weight by listening to tapes will probably not succeed.
4. A. tosses it
   C. offers it
5. D. can have a subtle, short-lived impact on perceptions
6. A. People have a better opinion of shapes they have seen before.

Listening: Scoring Information

■ For each of the six multiple-choice questions, a correct answer ➜ 1 point.

Total possible in listening section: 6

Add your points. This is your raw score. Use the conversion table to convert your raw score to one similar to a TOEFL® score.

Listening Score Conversion	
Raw Score	**Converted Score**
6	30
5	23
4	17
3	9
2	3
1	0
0	0

Speaking (page 74)

Rate each element of the response using the scoring charts. Then follow the directions to estimate your score.

Question 1: Telecommuting (independent speaking task)

Is there a clear statement of the main idea?	0	1	2	3	4
Are there specific ideas that support the main idea?	0	1	2	3	4
Are the ideas organized logically?	0	1	2	3	4
Is the information relevant and complete?	0	1	2	3	4
Is the grammar understandable and correct?	0	1	2	3	4
Is vocabulary correct and varied?	0	1	2	3	4
Is pronunciation clear and understandable?	0	1	2	3	4
Is the speech smooth and flowing?	0	1	2	3	4

This speaking question is worth 4 points. Add your points from each row. Divide the total by 8. Round to the nearest half-point; for scores ending in .25 or .75, round up.

Question 1 Raw Score: _____ (0–4)

Question 2: Privacy (integrated speaking task)

Is there a clear statement of the main idea or an organizing statement?	0	1	2	3	4
Does the speaker incorporate information from both the reading and the listening?	0	1	2	3	4
Does the speaker give an accurate summary of the information?	0	1	2	3	4
Does the speaker use time effectively?	0	1	2	3	4
Is the grammar understandable and correct?	0	1	2	3	4
Is vocabulary correct and varied?	0	1	2	3	4
Is pronunciation clear and understandable?	0	1	2	3	4
Is the speech smooth and flowing?	0	1	2	3	4

This speaking question is worth 4 points. Add your points from each row. Divide the total by 8. Round to the nearest half-point; for scores ending in .25 or .75, round up.

Question 2 Raw Score: _____ **(0–4)**

Question 3: Roosevelt and Churchill (integrated speaking task)

Is there a clear statement of the main idea or an organizing statement?	0	1	2	3	4
Does the speaker give an accurate summary of the information?	0	1	2	3	4
Does the speaker use time effectively?	0	1	2	3	4
Is the grammar understandable and correct?	0	1	2	3	4
Is vocabulary correct and varied?	0	1	2	3	4
Is pronunciation clear and understandable?	0	1	2	3	4
Is the speech smooth and flowing?	0	1	2	3	4

This speaking question is worth 4 points. Add your points from each row. Divide the total by 7. Round to the nearest half-point; for scores ending in .25 or .75, round up.

Question 3 Raw Score: _____ **(0–4)**

Add your raw scores for the three speaking questions. Round up for any half points. (For example, 9.5 becomes 10.) Your raw score will be between 0 and 12 points. Use the conversion table to convert your raw score to one similar to a TOEFL® score.

Speaking Score Conversion	
Raw Score	**Converted Score**
12	30
11	27
10	24
9	20
8	18
7	15
6	12
5	9
4	5
3	2
2	1
1	0
0	0

Your Score for Speaking: _____

Sample responses can be heard on the audio CD (Tracks 48–50). Transcripts of these responses follow.

Question 1. Even though I can see why many people would want to work from home, I would choose to go in to my office every day to work. I think social interaction, um, interacting with people is a very important part of a job, and if you work from home, you miss this. I like to talk to my co-workers, not just to be friendly, but also to learn things from them and make myself a better employee. It's much harder to discuss something or make sure you understand someone if you are using email or telephone. Better to sit there next to them. And some jobs need some equipment, even just a fax or special computers, that is easier and less expensive to have access to in the office.

Question 2. A right to privacy means being allowed to keep information and other personal things private. In the United States, the government says people have a right to privacy, and a right to raise children and live how you want. But sometimes the government says that other things are more important, like a right of the police to search your house if they think you're a criminal. It can be very difficult to decide whose rights are more important if there is conflict. Sometimes a person wants to keep a secret . . . that, um, the reporters want to publish in a newspaper. Maybe famous people and people in politics have this problem a lot, and it is hard to decide. How much should the reporters know about their personal life, and how much should their personal lives affect their careers? The right to privacy based on the Constitution is to protect everyone.

Question 3. The relationship between Roosevelt and Churchill seems friendly, but it is impossible to know for sure. The relationship between them was important because, uh, like the history professor says, . . . we can wonder if it had a lot to do with ending World War II. Roosevelt and Churchill had to work together to win against Germany in North Africa, and to free Europe from the control of Hitler. But were they friends doing this? We know about their friendship mostly from what Churchill writes in his book and, of course, he might have, might write that for his own reasons. But Churchill did not go to Roosevelt's funeral, which I believe a close friend would do. So, um, maybe they were not close friends, or they could have been just good leaders who are working together . . . they worked together well, but they were not really friends. The professor makes a point that the personalities of the two men must be important, and so it could be that they worked so well together and accomplished good things because of a real friendship.

Writing (page 77)

Rate each element of the response using the scoring chart. Then follow the directions to estimate your score.

Integrated writing task

Does the response do what the prompt asks for?	0	1	2	3	4	5
Is there a clear thesis statement?	0	1	2	3	4	5
Are there specific ideas that support the thesis?	0	1	2	3	4	5
Does the writer incorporate information from both the reading and the lecture?	0	1	2	3	4	5
Does the writer accurately interpret information from the reading and lecture?	0	1	2	3	4	5
Are the ideas organized logically?	0	1	2	3	4	5
Is the information relevant and complete?	0	1	2	3	4	5
Are sentences grammatically correct using a variety of sentence types?	0	1	2	3	4	5
Is vocabulary correct and appropriate to the topic?	0	1	2	3	4	5
Are transitions logical and smooth?	0	1	2	3	4	5

This writing question is worth 5 points. Add your points from each row. Divide the total by 10.

Raw Score: _____ (0–5)

Use the conversion table to convert your raw score to one similar to a TOEFL® score.

Writing Score Conversion	
Raw Score	Converted Score
5.0	30
4.5	26
4.0	22
3.5	20
3.0	17
2.5	13
2.0	8
1.5	3
1.0	1
0	0

Your Score for Writing: _____

A sample response follows.

Though both sources discuss dispute resolution, the lecture casts doubt on the reading's positive portrayal of adversarial procedures. The lecture points out problems with them and says that alternative dispute resolution (ADR) is a superior way of resolving legal contests.

The reading suggests that the adversarial procedures of the U.S. legal system are the best option for dispute resolution. The reading speaks favorably of the simplicity of an adversarial procedure. It has limited outcomes, the reading says, and it reduces a complex situation to one core issue. The reading says this helps clarify disputes.

According to the lecture, this simplicity can be a bad thing. It unnecessarily limits creativity in finding solutions for problems. ADR deals more flexibly with complex situations. ADR can approach a problem as having many sides, not just as one core issue with only two possible outcomes.

ADR does not treat a dispute as a zero-sum game. In other words, ADR can lead to a resolution without there necessarily being a winner and a loser. Instead both parties can find satisfaction because the outcome is not an either/or situation. The settlement can be beneficial to both sides. Also, because ADR does not require a court proceeding, it costs far less than a traditional legal trial.

(209 words)

Total Score

Add the four converted scores: reading, listening, speaking, and writing. The TOEFL® iBT is worth 120 points. _____

AUDIO TRANSCRIPTS

Mini–Test 1

Listening (page 6)

Track 2

Listen to part of a lecture from a biology class. Answer the questions. Use your notes to help you. You have 8 minutes to complete the questions.

Drosophila melanogaster. It sounds like a monster from an old movie, doesn't it? Well, it's not nearly so scary. No. It's harmless, really. Just a little old fruit fly. *Drosophila melanogaster*—that's the scientific name for a fruit fly.

As it turns out, fruit flies are a very popular little pet for geneticists and biologists. Well, like a pet, I mean. And why do they like fruit flies so much? Well, geneticists like to study fruit flies for a whole bunch of reasons. They've been studying fruit flies for decades, actually, for more than a century now.

So, let's look at some of the main reasons why the fruit fly is so popular in the study of genetics. But before we do that, there's something important that you need to understand here. And that is the *assumption* behind the study of fruit flies. You see, genetic study relies on the principle that genetic principles are *universal.* This means that when you study fruit flies, you learn about genes in *all living species.* So the principles of genetics are thought to be universal. In other words, the laws of genetics apply to all living things: You study a pea, you can learn about an apple. And so on.

So, now, let's turn to the fruit fly. One of the reasons that scientists like to study fruit flies is just historical. You see, a lot is already known about the fruit fly. People have been studying it for a long time. I already mentioned that. And because of that, we have a lot of information about the fruit fly. For example—and this is not a minor point—the entire genome for the fruit fly has been almost entirely sequenced. I mean, a few questions remain, but basically, scientists know almost the whole line-up of genomes. There are only two other species for which we know the sequence of genomes, and those are the mosquito and the honeybee.

Second, the life cycle of fruit flies makes it very easy to handle. Their lives are short—just two weeks. They are very easy to breed. A single female can lay several hundred eggs, and those develop into adults within just 12 days. So, a geneticist can study several generations of flies in just a few months.

Also, fruit flies are very easy to keep in a lab. They are small, so they don't take up a lot of room in a laboratory. They're inexpensive; they're easy to keep in very large numbers.

Last, but not least, fruit flies have variations in certain inherited traits. Like eye color and wing formation. So scientists like to study these. And they can easily observe this variation under a microscope.

Oh, and then, as you read in Mendel's study, *Drosophila melanogaster* has a couple more magic little features. One is, she has just four pairs of chromosomes, although most of the action occurs on just three of these four. And these chromosomes are relatively thick, with a pattern of dark and light bands, so they can be seen under a microscope. So it's fairly easy to see what part of the chromosome you're looking at.

So, does this make sense? I mean, I really just can't say enough good things about the fruit fly. Oh, and it's not just in genetics that the fruit fly is used. Originally, that was its main use. But more and more, it's being studied in developmental biology, where they're looking to see how a complex organism arises from a simple fertilized egg. They're really focusing on the embryo, the embryonic development.

Speaking (page 8)

Track 3

Question 1. Listen to the question, and then give a spoken response. You have 15 seconds to prepare your response and 45 seconds to respond. Begin preparing your response after the beep.

> Think about the qualities of a good friend. Describe those qualities. Give specific examples and details in your response.

Track 4

Question 2. Read a short passage on a university-related topic, and then listen to a talk on the same topic. You have 45 seconds to read the passage. The recording will be about 30 seconds in length. Respond using information from both the reading and the talk. You have 30 seconds to prepare your response and 60 seconds to respond. Begin preparing your response after the beep that follows the question.

> You have reached the Student Services Comment Line. Please be sure to state the topic of your message. Speak after the tone: *beeeeeep.*

Um, hello. I just found out that the university is planning to close some of its computer labs. I understand that the school has to save money, but I don't think this idea is good for students. I mean, many students do come to campus with their own computers, but we don't bring our own printers, and some students don't even own printers. So, a lot of students use the computing centers' printers to print out papers. The wait for a printer is already long enough. Also, closing the centers earlier on Friday and Saturday nights will just make problems worse. In fact, weekend nights are often the best times to get a printer without a long wait. And what about the students who can't afford their own computers? This decision seems to favor students who have more money because those students can go out and buy all the computer equipment they need.

[PAUSE]

The student gives her comments on the new university policy to close computing centers or cut their hours. Summarize her opinion, and state her reasons for holding that point of view.

Track 5

Question 3. Listen to a conversation between a profession and a student. Then listen to the question. Respond using information from the conversation. You have 20 seconds to prepare your response and 60 seconds to respond. Begin preparing your response after the beep.

S: Hello, Professor Barker.

P: Hi, Melania. What can I help you with?

S: I am thinking of changing my major, but I wanted to get your advice.

P: Sure.

S: Well, when I first came to university, I planned to become a teacher. But I'm finding some of my teacher education courses to be a little bit boring. Then, I took your Journalism 101 and 102, just to fill some credits. I loved those courses, and I think I did pretty well in them.

P: In fact, you did exceptionally well.

S: I have already taken so many education courses that if I changed majors now, I'd have to graduate late.

P: Well, I think the real question is, What do you want to do after college? Do you want to be a teacher, or do you want to work in journalism?

S: I'm not totally sure. I don't know much about careers in journalism. And if I change majors now, it will be so expensive.

P: Well, Melania, it's up to you. Have you ever thought of doing an internship at a local newspaper to understand the career better? Or, have you ever thought about doing a double major? You could even complete your degree in education first and continue in night classes toward a second degree.

S: Hmmm. There's a lot to think about.

[PAUSE]

Briefly describe the student's problem and the solutions that are suggested. What do you think the student should do and why?

Mini–Test 2

Listening (page 18)

Track 6

Listen to a conversation between two students. Answer the questions. Use your notes to help you. You have 8 minutes to complete the questions.

F: Um, do you guys have, like, equipment, balls and stuff, that we can take outside the building?

M: Some equipment can be taken outside the building, including some balls. It can be checked out for a three-hour period. All equipment needs to be returned in its original condition.

F: Well, like, there's a bunch of us out on the south field, and we just want to play soccer and stuff. The goals aren't even up.

M: No, we're getting new ones. In fact, they're scheduled to be installed next week.

F: I mean, we need everything. We just decided to play, sort of a pick-up game. We don't even have a ball.

M: Well, lucky for you, we have everything you need: a ball, cones to make a goal and mark the field. We have some jerseys. Pinnies.

F: Yeah, yeah. That's perfect. That's what we need. Can I get all that stuff? I mean, it's free, right? That's what we need.

M: It's free of charge for three hours' use to each group.

F: Yeah, okay, good.

M: Okay, and I'll need to see your student I.D.

F: Sure, um, okay, yeah, uh, it should be . . . oh man, it's downstairs in my locker. Can I just give you my student number?

M: Your student number is sufficient together with a piece of photo I.D.—a driver's license maybe? We need something to hold the equipment.

F: Oh, man, that's all downstairs in my locker. What a nuisance. Well, I guess I can run down and grab it.

M: Do you want everything? The cones, jerseys, ball?

F: Uh, yeah, cones are good. And the ball. But we don't need those jerseys. No extra stuff. Yeah, just the cones, and the ball is what we really need. Can I just get the ball with no I.D.? I know the director, Charlene, and we could . . . .

M: (laughs) Charlene knows everybody, but that's not our system for checking equipment out. Sorry.

F: No, I get it. I see. Okay, I'll be right back in just a minute. Wait here.

M: Sure. I'll get your equipment ready.

Track 7

Question 4. Listen again to part of the conversation. Then answer the question.

M: (laughs) Charlene knows everybody, but that's not our system for checking equipment out. Sorry.

What does the man mean when he says, "Charlene knows everybody"?

Speaking (page 20)

Track 8

Question 1. Listen to the question, and then give a spoken response. You have 15 seconds to prepare your response and 45 seconds to respond. Begin preparing your response after the beep.

In many high schools, life-skills courses—such as money management, cooking, and basic car repair—are required. Other high schools do not require them. Should such courses be required in all high schools? Please give specific reasons to support your opinion.

Track 9

Question 2. Read a short passage on a university-related topic, and then listen to a talk on the same topic. You have 45 seconds to read the passage. The recording will be about 30 seconds in length. Respond using information from both the reading and the talk. You have 30 seconds to prepare your response and 60 seconds to respond. Begin preparing your response after the beep.

The term *hero* is often used loosely to mean "someone I admire." You might hear someone say, for example, "Tiger Woods is my hero." This does not cast Tiger Woods as a classic hero, a champion for good over evil. After all, he just plays golf. Still, for those who admire his golf skills or athleticism, Tiger Woods may be a personal hero.

Even leaders who achieve great things in more serious pursuits are not necessarily classic heroes. Napoleon Bonaparte, for example, led French forces throughout Europe and all the way to the frontiers of Russia. His deeds were beyond the scope of ordinary experience. But were they heroic? At the time of his conquest, most French people probably thought so. So he was a local hero. But is attacking and conquering one's neighbors for riches, or fame, or national glory really heroic in the true sense of "heroism"?

Compiling a list of real heroes is actually very difficult, partly because so few people accomplish truly great things for noble reasons. Mohandas Gandhi, perhaps. Maybe Albert Einstein or Mother Teresa. True heroism is a lot more common in stories or myths than in real life. The hero sacrifices for something—there's the moral side of it, something that raises the hero above an ordinary human.

[PAUSE]

The professor describes some common applications of the term *hero* to real individuals. Explain the differences among a personal hero, a local hero, and a classic hero.

Track 10

Question 3. Listen to part of a lecture from a geology class. Then listen to the question. Respond using information from the lecture. You have 20 seconds to prepare your response and 60 seconds to respond. Begin preparing your response after the beep.

The glaciers of the Midwest left behind soils and landscape features that support different plant communities. Glaciers picked up lots of dirt as they moved forward during the ice ages. After the weather warmed and the glaciers melted back, they deposited this material on the lands they covered. Earth deposited by receding glaciers falls into several categories, each of which favors different types of plant communities.

If the soil left by a glacier is rocky or sandy, it is called glacial till. Water drains quickly through it. Plant roots do not have enough time to absorb the water. Consequently, plants growing in till soils must tolerate dryness. Black oak trees and many grasses can do so.

Soil made mostly of smaller particles such as clay or silt holds more moisture and nutrients. These soils are neither very dry nor very wet. These soils typically support plant communities of red oak, pine, and birch trees.

Other soils are made mostly of clay and hold even more water. On such wet, clay-rich soils in the Midwest, a maple-beech forest or a hemlock forest may thrive. Such smaller plants as blueberry, blackberry, and skunk cabbage are usually mixed in.

[PAUSE]

Using information from the lecture, explain the differences among the three types of soils left by glaciers.

Track 11

Writing. Listen to part of a lecture on the topic you just read about.

The philosophies and achievements of the Greeks and Chinese of 2,500 years ago were remarkably different, as were their very views of themselves. The Greeks, more than any other ancient peoples, had a strong sense that people were in charge of their own lives. Greeks saw themselves as individuals, free to act as they chose. The Greeks explored these ideas in their representations of life through art, literature, and sculpture.

The Chinese were not so worried about philosophical issues of control by others or the environment. They did not focus so heavily on the freedom of the individual. Instead, the Chinese focused on creating a harmonious social structure. The Greeks philosophized, while the Chinese emphasized the creation of practical tools for a productive society.

With this focus, Chinese civilization developed its technological know-how far beyond that of Greek civilization. The Chinese have been credited with the original invention of irrigation systems. Likewise, they developed ink, porcelain, and the magnetic compass. In shipping, the Chinese developed efficient new systems for powering and steering vessels. These technological achievements showed the effectiveness of the Chinese focus on practical matters.

[PAUSE]

Using examples and points from the lecture and reading, explain how the priorities of Greek and Chinese civilizations influenced the achievements of each.

Mini–Test 3

Listening (page 30)

Track 12

Listen to part of a lecture from a sociology class. Answer the questions. Use your notes to help you. You have 8 minutes to complete the questions.

The history of gambling in the United States is often thought of as falling into three main eras. The first period of gambling extends from the 1600s to the mid-1800s. Next is from the mid-1800s to the 1930s. The final period, which began in the 1930s, continues to this day. Today, let's look at the first period of gambling history.

But before we go on, let's set up a working definition of this word *gambling*. Gambling is any betting or wagering where the outcome is uncertain, or where the result depends on chance or skill. So, you could bet on a basketball game, a dogfight, or a roll of the dice.

Gambling is nothing new to mankind—humankind, that is. It's been around since ancient times. Archeologists have unearthed gambling bones and dice that date back to 40,000 CE. In fact, gambling has probably been around even longer than that. Anyway, Western forms of gambling came to the New World with the first colonists from Europe. This crowd brought with them cards, dice, and gaming tables. But it wasn't just home-gambling games they brought.

All of the original 13 colonies had lotteries. They used these lotteries to raise money, which helped pay for some of America's most prestigious schools—Harvard, Yale, Dartmouth, Columbia, Princeton. Lottery monies were also used to build churches and libraries, roads and hospitals. In fact, in 1823, Congress approved a lottery to pay for the beautification of Washington, DC. That didn't quite work out because the organizers made off with the money. It's worth noting here that England fought, on and off, to control lotteries in the colonies. At one point, the Crown wanted to ban lotteries. This built the lotteries up into a symbol of the fight for independence.

As America expanded, so did gambling—horse racing, cockfights, dogfights. And by the early 1800s, there were casinos, too, and these flourished, especially in the South. Southerners generally tolerated gaming, and the Mississippi River Valley became a hotbed for gamblers. These were legal, legitimate, organized operations, many of them centered in New Orleans.

This was sort of the Hollywood version of gambling. Colorful characters, lavish steamboats, that sort of thing. Travelers, merchants, and professional gamblers rode the rivers looking for action. Now the South's tolerance for gambling started weakening as professional gamblers—people who saw it as a job—became more common. These professional gamblers were seen as dishonest, and the local citizens fought against them. In fact, in 1835, a citizen group captured and executed five professional card players in Mississippi. This scared away other professional gamblers, and many of them traveled west.

There were other factors, too, that forced the end of Mississippi gambling, in particular, the emergence of the railroad. Travel by steamboat along the Mississippi River was being replaced by trains, which were, of course, faster and more reliable. Then the Civil War suddenly interrupted all river travel, nearly bringing gambling there to a halt.

Not just river gambling, but an entire era, was slowly coming to an end. Even the lotteries were starting to lose respect, surrounded by scandal and corruption. In 1833, Pennsylvania, New York, and Maryland all ended their legal state lotteries. By 1840, most states had banned them completely. By the mid-1800s, legal gambling was limited mostly to fancy clubs in New York, and, of course, horse racing, which, of all forms of legal gambling, has remained the most socially acceptable throughout the history of Europeans in North America.

The second major wave of gambling that historians discuss began in the mid-1800s, with a new focus on the West. We'll pick up here after the break.

Track 13

Question 2: Listen again to part of the lecture. Then answer the question.

> This was sort of the Hollywood version of gambling.

> What does the professor mean when he refers to "the Hollywood version of gambling"?

Speaking (page 33)

Track 14

Question 1. Listen to the question, and then give a spoken response. You have 15 seconds to prepare your response and 45 seconds to repond. Begin preparing your response after the beep.

Think of experiences in your life that have taught you something you could not have learned in school. Describe one such experience, and explain how it was instructive.

Track 15

Question 2. Read a short passage on a university-related topic, and then listen to a conversation on the same topic. You have 45 seconds to read the passage. The recording will be about 30 seconds in length. Respond using information from both the reading and the conversation. You have 30 seconds to prepare your response and 60 seconds to respond. Begin preparing your response after the beep.

F1: We should go to this WalkFest thing on Friday.

F2: This what?

F1: Here. Look at this flyer.

F2: Hmmm . . . okay. . . . .That's ridiculous. Three miles a day? That's impossible. I can't do that.

F1: Oh, come on, Sue. You probably walk almost that far already just going from one building to another on campus.

F2: Maybe you do, but I am not an athlete or good at sports. I believe in saving my energy for other things.

F1: Sue, you don't have to be athletic. It's not a race. Nobody cares how fast you walk.

F2: Also, I don't really wear walking shoes very much. Sandals or flip-flops go a lot better with the clothes I like.

F1: So you'd let fashion keep you from being healthy?

F2: Absolutely.

F1: But we should go to the launch anyway and sign up. You get free stuff.

F2: I'm never going to read that book. And a pedometer? Why do I want one of those?

F1: Don't you think it would be fun just to find out how far you're already walking?

F2: No. I don't care about things like that. Plus, I've got a class on Friday at noon.

[PAUSE]

Sue gives her opinion of walking for the school's WalkFest campaign. State her opinion and the reasons she gives for holding that opinion.

Track 16

Question 3. Listen to a conversation between two students. Then listen to the question. Respond using information from the conversation. You have 20 seconds to prepare your response and 60 seconds to respond. Begin preparing your reponse after the beep.

F: Excuse me, but I need some help.

M: Yes, how can I help you?

F: I bought this software here last week, and it doesn't work on my computer.

M: Okay, can you tell me what happened when you tried to load it onto your computer?

F: I put the CD in my computer, and a dialog box came up saying it was ready to install it, and then my screen went black and nothing happened. It took me a while, but I got the CD out. I rebooted my computer, and then everything was back to normal, I think.

M: That isn't supposed to happen. Maybe your computer isn't compatible with this software.

F: I have one of the models listed on the software box.

M: That's good. Then I think the problem is with your computer, not the software.

F: What should I do then?

M: You have a few options. I can exchange this one for another copy of the software, and you can try it again on your computer, just in case there is a problem with this particular CD. If it works this time, then everything is probably fine with your computer. Or, you can wait for me to run some tests on this CD, and if it comes up as okay, then you should consider taking your computer to one of the repair shops and have them take a look at it. Tell them what happened.

F: Okay, let me think about it. Thanks for your help.

[PAUSE]

Briefly describe the problem and the solutions offered. What do you think the student should do and why?

Writing (page 36)

Track 17

Listen to part of a lecture on the topic you just read about.

Oatmeal is a type of cereal made from the crushed and dried grains of oat plants. During the 1980s, it became the centerpiece of several fat diets, many of which made wild claims about the benefits of oatmeal. There was science behind most of these claims, as oatmeal can be shown to improve digestion and provide important nutrients. However, many diet promoters went beyond the science to claim that oatmeal could make stupid people smart, turn clumsy people into athletes, and even make unpleasant people nicer. It was said to help prevent cancer of the skin and of the digestive system.

Not much was said, however, about the potential dangers in high-oatmeal diets. For example, people who are allergic to wheat are also likely to be allergic to oatmeal. There is also a danger that consumers will forget that an average serving of oatmeal contains 150 to 200 calories. As with any food, eating too much of it can make you overweight. And the focus on one food in a diet is disturbing. Anyone who loads up on the nutrients in one food is likely to ignore other equally healthy foods. And that's what we need—a balance of nutrients in the human body.

One might ask what motivated the promoters of these dramatic oatmeal diets. After all, it's a simple food, extremely cheap, and easily available. No one is likely to get rich selling designer oatmeal. No, the attraction for diet promoters was in selling products that capitalized on oatmeal's popularity: diet books, motivational videos, the perfect kitchen ware, that sort of thing. In other words, marketers were trying to cash in on oatmeal paraphernalia.

[PAUSE]

Summarize the points made in the lecture, explaining how they cast doubt on points made in the reading.

Mini–Test 4

Listening (page 45)

Track 18

Listen to part of a conversation between two students. Answer the questions. Use your notes to help you. You have 8 minutes to complete the questions.

M: Hey, did you look at King's syllabus?

F: King? Oh, yeah, anthropology?

M: Yeah, aren't you taking that, too?

F: Yeah, I am. But I haven't checked the syllabus yet. What, did you get it online?

M: Yeah, you should check it out. There's some stuff in there where you can choose, like, to do a class presentation or a portfolio. You get a choice. Stuff like that.

F: Oh yeah? I hate presentations. I wonder what he wants in that portfolio.

M: I don't know. It didn't say a lot about portfolios. It's mostly, like, a collection of your work. Just a binder or something. I mean, not all of your work. It's supposed to represent your best work. You can put in newspaper articles or other research. It's something you're supposed to be proud of. You can show it off. You know, like artists have.

F: Yeah, I know what a portfolio is. We did them in one of my English classes in high school. There was a lot of neat stuff.

M: Do you still have yours?

F: Somewhere. Probably my parents' basement. But I wouldn't show it to anyone, I mean, it's not an example of anything. Still, it was kind of fun, and I've kept it, I think. Most of my work from high school just ended up in a trash bin somewhere.

M: Yeah, so there's those portfolios, and then there's one other biggie. The final exam is optional. I mean you have a choice. You can take the final exam, or you can do a longer paper.

F: What does that mean, "a longer paper"?

M: Well, there's the research paper—the famous research paper—and it's usually 25 or 30 pages in length, I guess. I mean, that's how long it usually is. But this semester, you have the option of doing more extensive research. That's what it says in the syllabus, "more extensive research." And if you choose that option, your final paper is supposed to be about twice as long. So, 50 or 60 pages.

F: And then you don't have to sit for the final?

M: I guess not. I mean, that's what the online syllabus says. It must be.

F: Wow. That sounds like a pretty good option. You could spread your work out then, over the term, and you wouldn't have to cram during finals week.

M: (laughs) Yeah, or you might end up cramming even more. Sixty pages isn't short.

F: That's true, but I mean, seriously, if you got a good start on it, you could be done long before finals week.

M: Well, I don't know. It sounds good to sit here and say that, but I'm not sure I'm up for writing a 60-page paper. I'd probably rather just go the old route. I mean, it's not just the writing. Writing is just part of it. It's the research that takes so much time. Searching online, setting up interviews, reading, compiling data. It's the research that sucks all your energy. The writing, though, I mean, even that, too . . . 60 pages is a lot.

F: Yeah, you're probably right. Plus, it all just depends. I mean, if I could find a really good research topic, that's one thing. But if you don't really find a good topic in the first place, there's no reason to turn it into 60 pages of anything.

M: (laughs) Well, that's for sure. I'll probably just take the final. Thirty pages is enough writing for me on any topic.

F: Maybe you're right. I'll have to learn more about this, though.

Speaking (page 47)

Track 19

Question 1. Listen to the question, and then give a spoken response. You have 15 seconds to prepare your response and 45 seconds to respond. Begin preparing your response after the beep.

If you could live for one year in a country other than your own, what country would it be and why?

Track 20

Question 2. Read a short passage on a university-related topic, and then listen to a talk on the same topic. You have 45 seconds to read the passage. The recording will be about 30 seconds in length. Respond using information from both the reading and the talk. You have 30 seconds to prepare your response and 60 seconds to respond. Begin preparing your response after the beep.

In taking a systematic look across a set of visionary companies, researchers found substantial evidence that these companies invested for the future to a greater degree than comparison companies. By analyzing financial statements dating back to the year 1915, researchers found that visionary companies consistently invested more heavily in new property, plants, and equipment as a percentage of annual sales than the comparison companies. They also put a greater percentage of each year's earnings back into the company, paying out less in cash dividends to shareholders. In addition, the visionary companies invested more heavily in research and development as a percentage of sales. The visionary companies also invested more aggressively in human capital through extensive recruiting, employee training, and professional development programs. Finally, the visionary companies invest earlier and more significantly in such aspects as technical know-how, new technologies, new management methods, and innovative industry practices. These companies did not wait for the world to impose the need for a change; they adopted the change ahead of many other companies.

[PAUSE]

Considering the information you have just received from the reading and the lecture, describe the characteristics of visionary companies.

Track 21

Question 3. Listen to part of a lecture from a zoology class. Then listen to the question. Respond using information from the lecture. You have 20 seconds to prepare your response and 60 seconds to respond. Begin preparing your response after the beep.

No group of animals depends more on healthy, specific habitats than butterflies. Butterflies need a diversity of species from which to feed as adults. At the same time, interestingly enough, they require specific larval host plants. These larval hosts are the plants that adult butterflies lay eggs on, and which ultimately become the food for the developing caterpillar. For instance, a female Monarch butterfly will lay eggs only on milkweed, but the butterfly herself feeds on the nectar of a wide variety of flowers.

So the question becomes *why* the larvae would have different feeding requirements from the mother. One might expect the answer to relate to genetics or nutritional needs or so on, but in fact, the research shows otherwise. As it turns out, at least part of a larva's taste for a certain plant seems to be its experience. Cabbage butterflies, for example, lay their eggs on cabbage plants. And cabbage butterfly larvae feed on the cabbage plant. If a larva is moved from a cabbage plant to a nasturtium plant, it will stop eating. Now, the nasturtium plant does produce several "antifeedants" to discourage cabbage butterfly larvae from consuming it. But the nasturtium leaves are not actually poisonous to the larvae. What's more interesting is that if we put the eggs of a cabbage butterfly on a nasturtium plant, and the eggs are allowed to develop there, those cabbage butterfly larvae will eat the nasturtium. So it appears that the eggs' presence on an original host plant can affect what the larvae are willing to eat. In other words, it seems that the conditions in which a larva was raised must have a big influence on its sensitivity to antifeedants.

[PAUSE]

Using the information presented in the lecture, describe the feeding habits of adult butterflies and butterfly larvae.

Mini–Test 5

Listening (page 57)

Track 22

Listen to part of a lecture and discussion from a health class. Answer the questions. Use your notes to help you. You have 8 minutes to complete the questions.

P: Okay, class, so let's do a quick review here from our last class. We were talking about food irradiation. Food irradiation is a process for treating food with ionizing radiation. And we talked about the purpose and function of irradiation, why we irradiate food. And the main reasons are, well, it kills bacteria in the food, and it can prolong the shelf life of some foods.

Today, we're going to talk a little bit about the process itself—the process of irradiation. And basically, there are three different ways. Three different irradiation technologies. They are one, gamma rays. Two, electron beams. And three, X-rays. Three ways.

First, we'll look at gamma rays. Gamma rays are produced by certain radioactive substances: cobalt 60 and cesium 137. You don't need to remember those. But what you do need to know is that these two elements are radioactive, and they give off gamma rays. Gamma rays are very effective for irradiation because they can penetrate foods to a depth of several feet.

Now, a lot of people, when they hear that their pineapple has been exposed to gamma rays, they worry. They worry that the rays will make their food radioactive. But this is not the case. Irradiation by gamma rays does not transfer radioactivity to the food. And there have been a lot of studies done on this topic. Yes, question?

S: Well, the irradiated food may not be made radioactive, but what about radioactive waste that results from this process?

P: That's a good question, and a fair one. Well, cobalt 60 is manufactured in a commercial nuclear reactor, and cesium 137 is a by-product of manufacturing weapons-grade radioactive substances. And both are handled as radioactive substances. That's true.

Of the two, from a safety standpoint, the cobalt is probably a little bit better. The cobalt used in irradiation decays by 50 percent in five years. That's a pretty short half-life. Cesium 137 has a half-life of just over 30 years. In addition, cobalt is a solid metal, so even if somehow it were to break, it would not spread in the environment. Cobalt is disposed of as a radioactive waste, but it is not considered highly problematic. Also, the cobalt pencils—they're called "pencils"—that are used in irradiation facilities, can be recharged at the original nuclear reactor. So, as far as radioactive waste goes, it's not too bad. Does that make sense?

S: Yes, but the cesium? What about cesium?

P: Well, cesium is a little different in that it is a soft metal that turns into a liquid at 83 degrees Fahrenheit—just above room temperature. Even at lower temperatures, it is powdery and can easily get into water or air. If some cesium 137 were to spill in an accident, or leak, for example, radioactive material could indeed spread into the environment. In fact, that happened some years ago in Georgia, at a medical sterilizer facility. Some of the cesium leaked into a water tank. That was a medical facility, so, as you can see, the gamma irradiation is used to sterilize medical and dental products, too. But anyway, we're getting a little off-track here.

Let's go on. The second way that food is irradiated is through electron beams. These beams are propelled through an electron gun. The gun propels high-energy electrons at the food to be treated. Now here, no radioactivity is involved. But the limitation here is that e-beams can penetrate food only to a depth of three centimeters—a little over an inch. That's *three centimeters*, compared to *three or four feet*.

Last of all is a newer technology called X-ray irradiation. This is the newest method of food irradiation, and it is still being developed. It's quite similar to e-beams in many ways, because it aims its beams at a target, but the electrons aren't aimed directly at the food. Instead, they are directed at a thin plate of gold or other metal. Excited by these electrons, the atoms in the gold plate give off X-rays, which then strike the food. X-rays can penetrate deeper than electrons, so it can be used to treat thicker foods. And again, no radioactivity. There are only a handful of commercial X-ray irradiation units around the world, because this technology is still pretty new.

Track 23

Question 4. Listen again to part of the lecture. Then answer the question.

Some of the cesium leaked into a water tank. That was a medical facility, so, as you can see, the gamma irradiation is used to sterilize medical and dental products, too. But anyway, we're getting a little off-track here.

What does the lecturer mean when she says, "we're getting a little off-track here"?

Speaking (page 60)

Track 24

Question 1. Listen to the question, and then give a spoken response. You have 15 seconds to prepare your response and 45 seconds to respond. Begin preparing your response after the beep.

Some volunteer work involves doing something directly for *people*, such as teaching someone to read or serving food. Other volunteers work mostly with *things*, such as preparing mailings or working on computers. What type of volunteer work do you prefer, and why? Give reasons to support your answer.

Track 25

Question 2. Read a short passage on a university-related topic, and then listen to a conversation on the same topic. You have 45 seconds to read the passage. The recording will be about 30 seconds in length. Respond using information from both the reading and the conversation. You have 30 seconds to prepare your response and 60 seconds to respond. Begin preparing your response after the beep.

M: Hey, I see you've got *The Namesake*. What do you think about having to read a book before we start classes?

F: Well, I'm excited to read the book. I think it's a good idea. I mean, we live in such a homogenous place. Everyone, mostly, is white, and we all go to the same few churches.

M: Yeah, but I'm not really sure I want to talk with strangers at the orientation about things like race and religion.

F: Well, it wouldn't bother me. Okay, forget about race and religion. What about economic groups?

M: What about them?

F: Well, the university has rich students, working-class students, poor students on scholarship. The whole range. Not like here—all middle-class people.

M: That's cool. But again . . . So we're in this orientation and somebody makes a remark about poor people and the poor people in the room start getting offended. . . .

F: You're too worried about it. This is college. People can take a few uncomfortable remarks.

M: Yeah, you're right. I think it could be a good introduction to college life.

[PAUSE]

Briefly describe the woman's view of the reading requirement and the topics that she expects to be discussed.

Track 26

Question 3. Listen to a conversation between a professor and a student. Then listen to the question. Respond using information from the conversation. You have 20 seconds to prepare your response and 60 seconds to respond. Begin preparing your response after the beep.

S: Hello, Professor Kaplan?

P: Yes, that's me. Come on in.

S: My name is Su Kyeong Hong, and I'm choosing my classes for winter quarter. I'd like to take your course, Poli-Sci 312, but it has a couple of prerequisites, or "permission of the instructor."

P: Yes, that course is, uh, U.S. Politics of the 20th Century. It has a couple of prereqs: a history of the United States, and then Poli-Sci 311, which is Political Development in the 18th and 19th Centuries.

S: Well, I've taken U.S. history, and I have a strong background in French politics.

P: Well, without Poli-Sci 311, 312 is a real challenge.

S: I am interested in taking 311, but it isn't offered again until next fall, and I'd like to get going in this series now, because next year I want to take the 411 series, and, (*laughs*), well as you know, the 300-series is a prereq for *that*.

P: Well, here's what I'll do. I can give you the course syllabus for Poli-Sci 311. You go through it and see if you feel comfortable with the topics. If you do, I'm willing to sign you into 312. But I don't want you to get in over your head.

S: Okay, I'll look at the syllabus and think about it. Thanks for your time.

[PAUSE]

Briefly describe the student's problem and the solutions that are suggested. What do you think the student should do and why?

Mini–Test 6

Track 27

Listening (page 71)

Listen to part of a lecture from a psychology class. Answer the questions. Use your notes to help you. You have 8 minutes to complete the questions.

Today, we are going to talk about subliminal perception, and in particular, we are going to talk about whether or not people's behavior can be manipulated by subliminal messages. What we want to know is whether people's actions can be influenced by information that they receive subliminally.

Okay, now, that's a lot of big words coming at you pretty fast. Let's slow down here, and we'll talk first about subliminal perception. What is subliminal perception? Subliminal perception is the perception of stimuli that are below our conscious awareness. For example, it could be a sound that is too faint for a person to hear consciously. It could be a visual image that is presented so quickly that a person can't consciously see or identify it.

Some of you may have heard of subliminal perception, and there are some common myths surrounding it. There's the famous story of the marketer who claimed that he increased the sales of popcorn and soda pop in a movie theater by flashing the words "eat popcorn" and "drink Coke" during the movie. That's a famous story, and for some reason, people like to repeat it. In fact, it was so interesting that it attracted researchers' interest, and they tried to replicate those claims. But they couldn't. Their controlled tests showed that people's behavior could not be significantly influenced by words embedded in movies, for example. And there have been lots of these tests. Again and again, they show that subliminal messages in advertising do not influence consumers' decisions. In other words, you can't listen to subliminal self-help tapes and expect to stop smoking. So, uh, I hope I haven't ruined any of your plans for losing weight.

But does that mean that subliminal stimuli have no influence on people? Well, not necessarily. But the effects of subliminal stimuli appear to be quite subtle. And researchers have set up several experiments to test this. For example, one researcher, named Morris Eagle, flashed images of a boy. Some of the subjects in his study saw images of the boy throwing a birthday cake angrily. Other subjects were presented images of the boy sweetly offering the cake to somebody. Later, Eagle showed all of the subjects a picture of the boy in a neutral position. In that case, those who had previously seen the boy throwing the cake judged the boy much more negatively than those who had seen the boy offering the cake to somebody else. In other words, the subjects' subliminal exposure to the boy's actions influenced how they evaluated the boy. However, studies repeatedly show that the effects of these subliminal studies are weak and short lived. There is no evidence that subliminal stimuli can change a person's behavior in any major or long-lasting way.

A similar area of research involves something called the *mere exposure effect*. This phenomenon relates to that fact that when people are repeatedly exposed to something new, such as a shape or image, their liking for that image will increase. For instance, researchers show a Chinese character subliminally to subjects over a period of time. These are, by the way, subjects who aren't familiar with Chinese characters. Anyway, later, they show the subjects several Chinese characters, and they ask them to pick their favorite one. In those studies, subjects are more likely to choose the character that was presented subliminally. So, to some degree, attitudes can be influenced by subliminal stimuli.

Track 28

Question 3. Listen again to part of the lecture. Then answer the question.

> In other words, you can't listen to subliminal self-help tapes and expect to stop smoking. So, uh, I hope I haven't ruined any of your plans for losing weight.

> What does the lecturer imply when he says, "I hope I haven't ruined any of your plans"?

Speaking (page 74)

Track 29

Question 1. Listen to the question, and then give a spoken response. You have 15 seconds to prepare your response and 45 seconds to respond. Begin preparing your response after the beep.

> Many companies now allow their employees to telecommute and work from home. If you were given this option, would you choose to work from home or go into the office to work? Give reasons to support your answer.

Track 30

Question 2. Read a short passage on a university-related topic, and then listen to a talk on the same topic. You have 45 seconds to read the passage. The recording will be about 30 seconds in length. Respond using information from both the reading and the talk. You have 30 seconds to prepare your response and 60 seconds to respond. Begin preparing your response after the beep.

> If you accept that there is a legal right to privacy, you also have to recognize the other interests that may override it. Whenever an invasion of privacy is claimed, there are usually competing values at stake. Privacy may seem paramount to a person who has lost it, but that right often clashes with other rights and responsibilities that a society deems important. The right to be secure in one's own home often collides with a police officer's need to investigate a crime. Our right to keep facts about ourselves secret often clashes with the concept of a free press. Which is more important, a homeowner's right to be secure against unwanted phone calls or a political candidate's right to ask for the homeowner's vote? The tradeoffs between privacy and competing social values or legal rights are different in each case. And sadly, much as Americans cherish privacy, it does not always triumph. There are many intrusions on privacy—telephone solicitations, junk mail, door-to-door evangelists, etc.—that may cause personal distress but are not legally actionable. Some such intrusions are deemed justifiable in order to let the press, police, social workers, employers, or others do their jobs.
>
> [PAUSE]
>
> Considering the information you have just received from the reading and the lecture, describe the right to privacy and some conflicts related to it.

Track 31

Question 3. Listen to part of a lecture from a history class. Then listen to the question. Respond using information from the talk. You have 20 seconds to prepare your response and 60 seconds to respond. Begin preparing your response after the beep.

Franklin Delano Roosevelt and Winston Churchill are routinely portrayed as personal friends—more than just allies. Their personal collaboration certainly made possible several of the turning points of World War II: the American decision to support Britain in its struggle against Germany in the months before Pearl Harbor; the victory over the Germans in the North African desert in 1942, which kept the Middle East out of Hitler's hands; the development and control of the atomic bomb; and the timing of the liberation of Europe.

While the concept of a Roosevelt-Churchill friendship lends a personal touch to this grueling era, some historians have called it nothing more than a convenient fiction. In this view, it was largely created by Churchill in his memoirs in an attempt to build an enduring U.S.-Britain alliance. Look, Churchill could have attended Roosevelt's funeral, but he chose not to. What was that about? Isn't it possible that the relationship was really nothing special—cordial and efficient but not much else? Some other U.S. president and British prime minister with no personal bond, the case continues, could just as well have produced the same results in World War II. Well . . . maybe, maybe not. I personally think this claim goes too far in depersonalizing things. I can't believe that the personalities of these two great men were so irrelevant. But, we'll never know for sure, I guess.

[PAUSE]

Using the information presented in the lecture, describe the relationship between Roosevelt and Churchill, and say why it was important.

Writing (page 77)

Track 32

Listen to part of a lecture on the topic you just read about.

Alternative dispute resolution (ADR) is a cooperative approach now being advocated by some overworked courts of law. The great benefit of it, if it works, is that it can reduce the cost of settling a lot of disputes. The disputing parties don't actually go to court, so they don't incur the legal fees they might otherwise have to pay. The ADR approach can also be more flexible than the courts in accommodating the disputants' underlying needs. For example, if two children are arguing over a piece of cake, it may seem obvious that the way to resolve the conflict is to cut the cake and give each child half. But this is not the best solution if one child likes the cake and the other likes the icing. In that case, each could get all of the part he or she likes best—if some moderator bothers to discover where the interests of each party really lie.

The key to success in such an approach is giving up an adversarial stance. An adversarial approach assumes that there is a single resource at issue, so either party's gain is the other party's loss. The basic assumption of adversarialism is that a dispute is a set of zero-sum games. I want Resource X, and so do you. One of us will win, and the other will lose. The same goes for Resources Y, Z, and so on. Even most searches for compromise are adversarial, based on the assumption that each party will start out by demanding more than they really expect and that they will eventually split the difference. In this spirit, a basic principle of negotiation is that lawyers should not reveal what their clients really want, because that might give the other side too much power.

ADR assumes no such zero-sum dynamics. We can both win. This encourages real negotiation and creativity, not the hardened, mutually incompatible positions that characterize adversarialism.

Even when everyone is civil and no one is abusive, the win-lose, two-sides structure of the adversarial system leads to bad solutions. Adversarialism reduces complex human problems to just two sides: Everyone must align with plaintiff or defendant. A problem-solving or mediation approach like ADR overcomes these drawbacks by providing for the participation of more than two sides.

[PAUSE]

Summarize the points made in the lecture, explaining how they cast doubt on points made in the reading.

Audioscripts of the sample speaking responses are found on pages 83–84, 91, 99, 108, 116, 124.

TRACK TABLE

Track 1: Copyright information

Mini–Test 1

Track 2: Listening
Track 3: Speaking Question 1
Track 4: Speaking Question 2
Track 5: Speaking Question 3

Mini–Test 2

Track 6: Listening
Track 7: Listening Question 4
Track 8: Speaking Question 1
Track 9: Speaking Question 2
Track 10: Speaking Question 3
Track 11: Writing

Mini–Test 3

Track 12: Listening
Track 13: Listening Question 2
Track 14: Speaking Question 1
Track 15: Speaking Question 2
Track 16: Speaking Question 3
Track 17: Writing

Mini–Test 4

Track 18: Listening
Track 19: Speaking Question 1
Track 20: Speaking Question 2
Track 21: Speaking Question 3

Mini–Test 5

Track 22: Listening
Track 23: Listening Question 4
Track 24: Speaking Question 1
Track 25: Speaking Question 2
Track 26: Speaking Question 3

Mini–Test 6

Track 27: Listening
Track 28: Listening Question 3

Track 29: Speaking Question 1
Track 30: Speaking Question 2
Track 31: Speaking Question 3
Track 32: Writing

Sample Speaking Responses

Mini–Test 1

Track 33: Question 1
Track 34: Question 2
Track 35: Question 3

Mini–Test 2

Track 36: Question 1
Track 37: Question 2
Track 38: Question 3

Mini–Test 3

Track 39: Question 1
Track 40: Question 2
Track 41: Question 3

Mini–Test 4

Track 42: Question 1
Track 43: Question 2
Track 44: Question 3

Mini–Test 5

Track 45: Question 1
Track 46: Question 2
Track 47: Question 3

Mini–Test 6

Track 48: Question 1
Track 49: Question 2
Track 50: Question 3